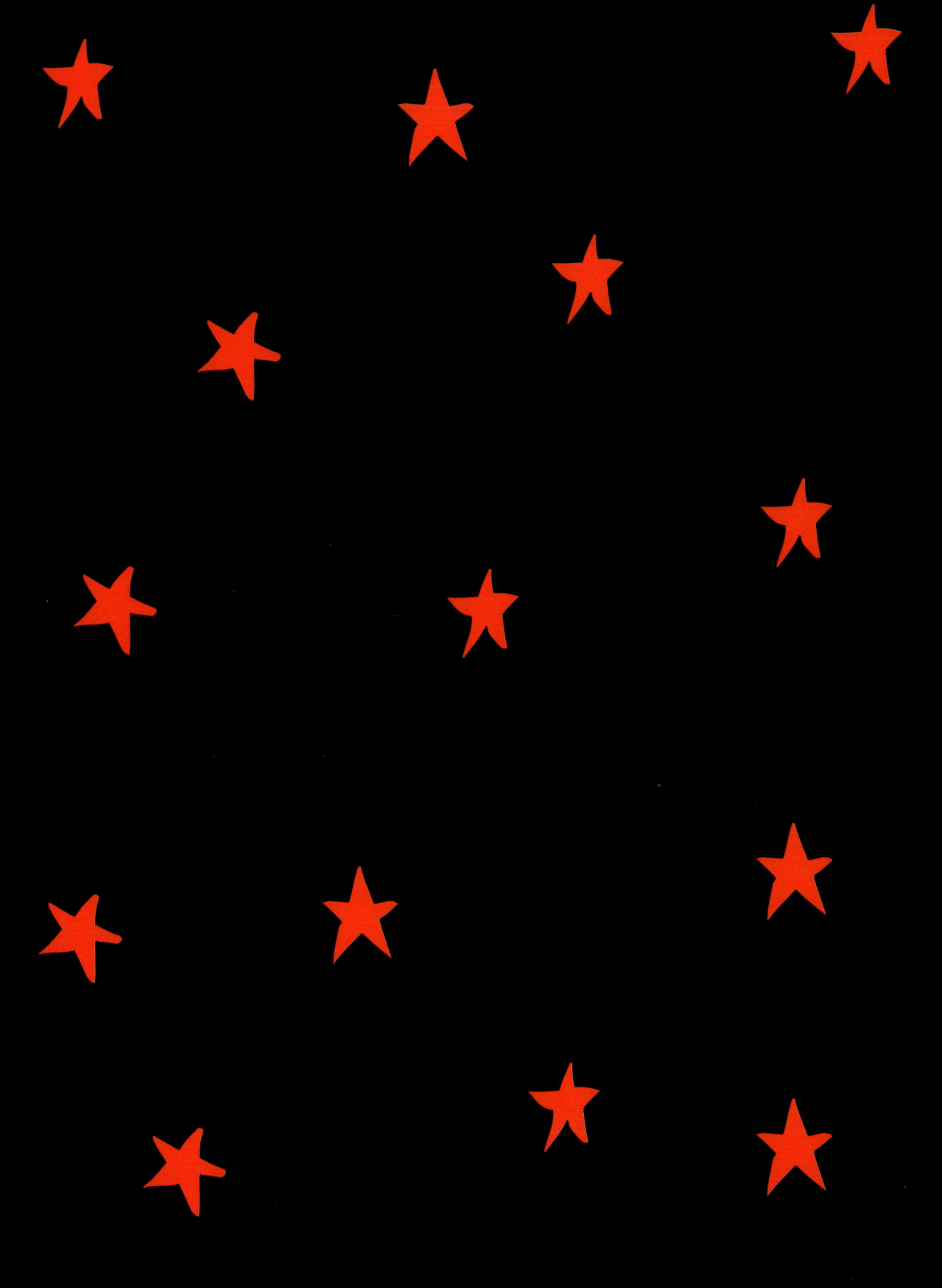

Aussie Rock Anthems

TOP 40

THE STORIES BEHIND OUR BIGGEST HIT SONGS

GLEN HUMPHRIES

[WARNING]

Aboriginal and Torres Strait Islander readers are advised that this book contains the names and voices of people who have died.

A Gelding Street Press book
An imprint of Rockpool Publishing
PO Box 252, Summer Hill
NSW 2130 Australia

www.geldingstreetpress.com
Follow us! @ geldingstreet_press

Published in 2024 by Gelding Street Press

Copyright text © Glen Humphries 2024
Copyright images © Tony Mott 2024
Copyright design © Gelding Street Press 2024

ISBN: 9781922662057

Author photo p. 227 by Warren Wheeler
Cover design by Alissa Dinallo
Internal design and typesetting by Sara Lindberg, Rockpool Publishing
Publisher: Luke West, Rockpool Publishing
Edited by Lisa Macken

All rights reserved. No part of this publication may be reproduced, stored in a retrieval system, or transmitted in any form or by any means, electronic, mechanical, photocopying, recording or otherwise, without the prior written permission of the publisher.

 A catalogue record for this book is available from the National Library of Australia

Printed and bound in China
10 9 8 7 6 5 4 3 2 1

TO KIM, WHO IS THE INSPIRATION BEHIND

INTRODUCTION   1

CHAPTER 1	Throw Your Arms Around Me, Hunters & Collectors	5
CHAPTER 2	Khe Sanh, Cold Chisel	13
CHAPTER 3	Beds are Burning, Midnight Oil	21
CHAPTER 4	It's A Long Way To The Top (If You Wanna Rock'n'Roll), AC/DC	31
CHAPTER 5	Working Class Man, Jimmy Barnes	41
CHAPTER 6	I Touch Myself, Divinyls	51
CHAPTER 7	Down Under, Men at Work	63
CHAPTER 8	Treaty, Yothu Yindi	71
CHAPTER 9	How To Make Gravy, Paul Kelly	83
CHAPTER 10	You're The Voice, John Farnham	91
CHAPTER 11	The Horses, Daryl Braithwaite	99
CHAPTER 12	Friday On My Mind, The Easybeats	103
CHAPTER 13	Sounds Of Then (This Is Australia), GANGgajang	107
CHAPTER 14	Scar, Missy Higgins	111
CHAPTER 15	Love Is In The Air, John Paul Young	115
CHAPTER 16	Am I Ever Gonna See Your Face Again, The Angels	119
CHAPTER 17	Berlin Chair, You Am I	123
CHAPTER 18	Don't Dream It's Over, Crowded House	127

CHAPTER 19	I Was Only 19 (A Walk In The Light Green), Redgum	131
CHAPTER 20	Get Free, The Vines	135
CHAPTER 21	Are You Gonna Be My Girl, Jet	139
CHAPTER 22	Great Southern Land, Icehouse	143
CHAPTER 23	Horror Movie, Skyhooks	147
CHAPTER 24	My Happiness, Powderfinger	151
CHAPTER 25	Eagle Rock, Daddy Cool	155
CHAPTER 26	April Sun In Cuba, Dragon	159
CHAPTER 27	Tomorrow, Silverchair	163
CHAPTER 28	Solid Rock, Goanna	167
CHAPTER 29	Shaddap You Face, Joe Dolce Music Theatre	171
CHAPTER 30	I Still Call Australia Home, Peter Allen	175
CHAPTER 31	My People, The Presets	179

AUSSIE ROCK ANTHEMS

CHAPTER 32	Howzat, Sherbet	183
CHAPTER 33	Buy Me A Pony, Spiderbait	187
CHAPTER 34	Can't Get You Out Of My Head, Kylie Minogue	193
CHAPTER 35	What About Me, Moving Pictures	197
CHAPTER 36	Somebody That I Used To Know, Gotye	201
CHAPTER 37	Prisoner Of Society, The Living End	205
CHAPTER 38	Blackfella/Whitefella, Warumpi Band	209
CHAPTER 39	Don't Change, INXS	213
CHAPTER 40	Boys Light Up, Australian Crawl	219

BIBLIOGRAPHY 223

ABOUT THE AUTHOR 227

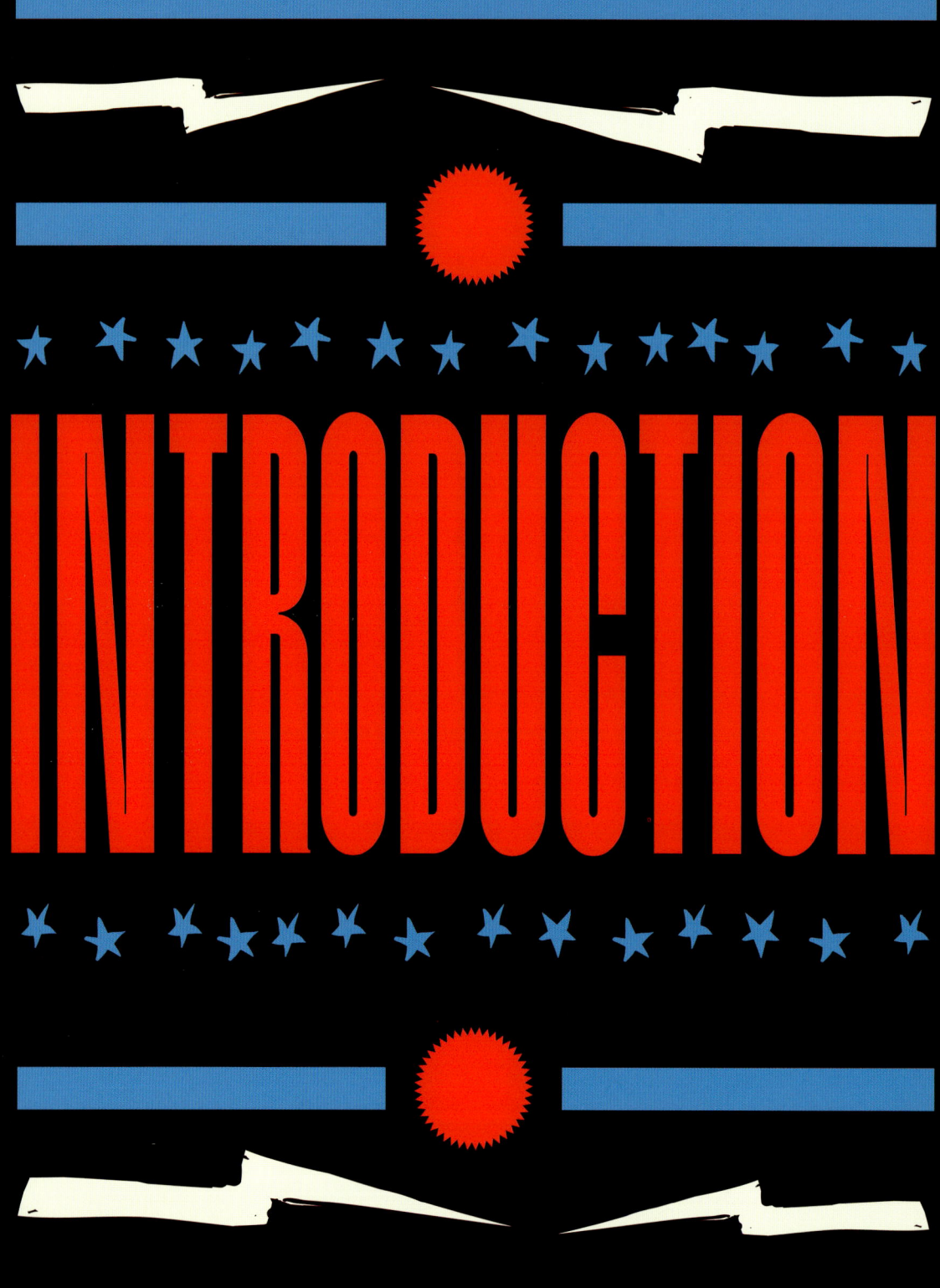

What a song is about and what you *think* it's about aren't always the same thing. One famous example of that is 'Every Breath You Take' by The Police, which some people have taken as an admission of eternal love, that whatever happens you'll be by their side; it gets played at weddings all the time. While it is love Sting's singing about, it's not a nice sort of love. It's the obsessive type – he's singing about someone stalking their ex.

There's also Bruce Springsteen's 'Born In The USA', which people have seen in a patriotic context when it's actually critical of America. The catchy pop of 'Semi-Charmed Life' by Third Eye Blind? That's about smoking crystal meth. When it comes to Australian songs, The Go-Betweens' 'Streets Of Your Town' is often seen as a fond ode to whatever town Grant McLennan was singing about, but that overlooks the dark references to domestic violence in the lyrics. Australian Crawl's hit 'Boys Light Up' is about . . . Well, you can find out at No. 40 in this book. Chances are it's not what you had assumed.

That's not necessarily wrong, because once a songwriter lets their work out into the wild they lose some ownership of it. They can't sit on the lounge next to you or the passenger seat of your car when you listen to the tune and tell you what it all means. They have to leave us to figure that out ourselves, and even if it's wrong it still works for us.

Some songwriters don't like their songs being misinterpreted, especially when it's used to support a cause or movement to which they are fundamentally opposed. Others are quite cool with people having their own interpretations, to the extent they're reluctant to spell out the truth behind a song. To their way of thinking it increases the chance a tune will resonate with a listener if they're allowed to create their own stories, even if it doesn't match the lyrics. That's all worth knowing right at the start: that your locked-in, rock-solid ideas of the subject matter of the songs that appear in the following pages may well be completely wrong, so don't be disappointed.

Something else worth knowing is that the songs on this list are all old: the newest song is 2011's 'Somebody That I Used To Know' by Gotye. There's a good reason why nothing new and hip and what the kids are listening to today are included here: by their very nature, iconic songs need the passage of time to be considered iconic. A song needs to show it can stand the test of time, that it can still be hanging around decades later. Five to 10 years isn't long enough to realise which songs resonated with us and which ones haven't.

If you do the maths, that means the vast bulk of these tunes came out in the last century, which goes some way to explaining a relative lack of female and First Nations artists: the Australian music scene then wasn't really blessed with a huge amount of diversity. If you weren't white and male you'd be pushing it uphill to get anywhere.

Thank Christ that's changed. If someone else writes a book like this 20 years from now the list will be way more diverse.

Speaking of lists, any time a list is created that ranks anything it's a certainty someone else will complain about why Thing X wasn't ranked higher or how come Thing Y missed out altogether. It therefore needs to be said that any ranking will always be arbitrary. A range of factors came into play when working out who would make the cut. Each artist could only appear once, so the top 40 didn't end up being clogged with Cold Chisel or AC/DC. Also, each song on the list had to pass the sing test, whereby you read the song title and, without a conscious decision on your part, you start singing the song in your head. Even if you don't like the band, an iconic song is one you've been exposed to so many times over the years: from radio stations to commercial jingles to the music that's piped into the supermarket while you push a trolley with wonky wheels around.

There were also other, more serious, deliberations. For instance, I felt a need to ensure both female and First Nations artists were represented in the top 10. And don't go on about that being woke: 'I Touch Myself' and 'Treaty' both deserve to be in the top 10, but so did a lot of other songs. Daryl Braithwaite's 'The Horses' was in the top 10 only to miss out right as I was putting the finishing touches on the book. The list isn't made up of songs I like, either: 'Eagle Rock' is one of the most annoying songs ever written by an Australian yet it made the cut, although I refused to listen to it while writing that chapter.

Likewise, people can make a case for any number of artists who should have made the cut. Should Olivia Newton-John have got a spot for 'Physical'? Yeah, probably, and as much as I dislike Air Supply (though to be honest that dislike is more muted the older I get), the tall blond and the dude with the afro wouldn't have been out of place in the top 40 either. Little River Band, Savage Garden, The Saints, Russell Morris, Rose Tattoo, Billy Thorpe, Slim Dusty – you could create a top 40 of artists who *didn't* get a look-in here.

While the title of this book includes the word 'rock', eagle-eyed music fans will notice that some of the 40 songs don't quite fit that description. Take Joe Dolce's 'Shaddup You Face': people have used all sorts of words to describe that song, some of which have been unkind, but no one would call it 'rock'. That song and a number of others have made the cut because of their significance to Australian music. Also, how can you have a book about the country's greatest songs and not include Kylie?

In the end, it should be about celebrating the great Australian music that *does* feature rather than bemoaning what missed out. If you do that, chances are you'll pull out the old vinyl – or flick on Spotify – and give some of these classics a listen. If you're going with the second option, I've helped you out a bit: search for 'Aussie Rock Anthems – The Playlist' to hear all 40 songs in order. ☀

INTRODUCTION

CHAPTER 1

Throw Your Arms Around Me

HUNTERS & COLLECTORS

The struggling musician knew there was something special about this weird, eclectic band from the other side of the world – so special that he brought Hunters & Collectors' first album along to the show to try to get it autographed. How he managed to get hold of it is anyone's guess; it's not like the Hunnas were a big deal in the United States in 1983.

It was a student gig in a San Diego club, and singer Mark Seymour remembered the band wasn't in the best mental space. A few members had quit, and it looked as though things might be about to break apart. 'The security guy knocks on the door and says there's this bloke outside that wants you to sign a record,' Seymour said. 'I was not really interested, but I went out, and it was a student gig so there were a lot of kids there.

'So a kid was there holding a record and said he was a big fan and asked if I could sign a record; pre [The] Jaws of Life, I think it was the first album. The album goes right around, everyone in the band signs it, I pass it back to him not knowing who it was and years later the rest is history.'

That guy was Eddie Vedder, later to make it big as the lead singer of Pearl Jam. He had a thing for Australian music, also being a fan of The Angels and Split Enz. He went on to cover 'Throw Your Arms Around Me', both with Pearl Jam and with Neil Finn for a Hunters & Collectors tribute album.

When he knocked on the stage door to get a few signatures, Hunters & Collectors were a very different beast to what they became with the iconic 'Throw Your Arms Around Me'. The band formed in 1981 out of the ashes of two other acts, The Jetsonnes and a perverse cover band called The Schnorts. The hybrid was a little bit weird: original member Greg Perano discovered a hot-water cylinder in the back yard of a house he used to live in, dragged it out in the light and took it to a band rehearsal. It became

To further complicate matters, all decisions were only ever reached by a majority vote, usually after long, dragged-out meetings. Songwriting was credited to all band members, regardless of how much various people contributed. Finally, there was also the issue of finances: having to split any cash at least seven ways was never going to result in making anyone rich. However, the upside to having so many members was that some of them had useful qualifications. Drummer Doug Falconer was a doctor, trombonist Michael Waters an accountant and bassist John Archer an engineer with a penchant for building big PA systems.

The band's music and image – well, that was weird too, which is to be expected if you have a water-cylinder player in the band. Sonically, it was loud, pounding, art school– and Talking Heads–inspired. Visually, the oddness of the band is on display in the video for 'Talking To A Stranger': amid the spooky, apocalyptic scenes is Seymour singing with rubber bands wrapped around his head and disfiguring his features.

known as 'The Wang', for the noise it made when percussionist Perano whacked it with a lump of metal.

There were a lot of people in the band, never any fewer than seven. When trumpeter Jack Howard turned up at a gig with a recording of a brass accompaniment to their song 'Talking To A Stranger' and handed it to Seymour, the Hunters soon added a brass section. Then there was the sound guy and artist Robert Miles, who was also part of the band and even appeared in album cover photos.

When you're a band in the late 1970s and early 1980s and you had an artistic bent you were beholden to go to Britain, because Australia was a cultural backwater that didn't know good music. So the band went to the UK, and it didn't go well at all. 'They literally came back with their tails very firmly between their legs. It was a disaster,' band

AUSSIE ROCK ANTHEMS

manager Michael Roberts said. 'A slightly different set of circumstances and the band could quite easily have finished.'

While in Europe the band recorded a second arty-themed album, *The Fireman's Curse*. It didn't capture much attention in Australia and, at the same time, caused their UK label to drop them. Perano, too, felt he'd had enough, and the band dissolved for a while before reforming to create 1984's *The Jaws of Life*. The arty side had been stripped away in preference for more of a rock feel, but it didn't see the band any steps up the ladder of success.

The band, as was their habit, had quite a few meetings to decide what to do next. At one of them, the subject of changing their style to get played on the radio and maybe having a few hit singles came up. 'I remember having a meeting at the Standard Hotel and talking to them, saying we have to make a commercial record,' Seymour said. 'And I remember consciously thinking, "I want to write pop songs." We gradually came round to realising that whatever kudos we had when we first started in the beginning of the 1980s, it was well and truly gone.'

If the band was to continue something had to change: the seven members couldn't keep going on recording albums that didn't sell. 'We made a conscious decision that we had to move beyond the inner suburbs if we were going to survive financially,' Roberts said. 'In terms of sustaining such a large group of people, you had to move out and play in the suburbs. That's a different beast altogether.'

That motivation inspired the video for the first single off what would be the *Human Frailty* album, 'Say Goodbye'. 'Mark with his head in the bonnet of a V8 was much more closely associated with the suburbs than it was with the inner city,' Roberts said.

The song that drove the band in this new direction was 'Throw Your Arms Around Me', which had first been released as a single back in November 1984 and which was re-recorded for *Human Frailty*. It was a song the band recorded at least four times in its career, because they could never manage to capture a definitive version on tape. Where the song thrives is in a live situation, where it gets stripped back to as few instruments as possible and resists the urge to add in sounds that can happen in the studio.

'Our manager got incredibly excited about it,' Seymour said. 'He could see the commercial mileage in it so he pushed us to record it again. One time we played it at the Palace Hotel to about 2000 people, who just went off. We finally got it right, so we recorded it again.'

The song was a bit of a left turn for the band, which had never before had Seymour present them with such an emotionally naked song. 'When Mark brought in the lyric for "Throw Your Arms Around Me" it was the first straight-up love song he'd ever written,' band drummer Falconer said. 'There were plenty of other songs before that

THROW YOUR ARMS AROUND ME 7

'I wrote virtually all of the lyrics on *Human Frailty* about my relationship with her,' Seymour said. 'She was a Van Morrison freak and that's when I discovered Van Morrison. She'd go off to work and I'd sit in the bungalow and listen to Van Morrison, exploring the idea of romance in music, which is something I'd never been that interested in. I'd become excited about music in the late 1970s through punk and new wave and romance had very little to do with that kind of music.'

The whole experience was a light-bulb moment for Seymour in terms of songwriting. Before then he felt the artistic side was something that had to be separated from yourself, that it had to be located away from whatever you were feeling. While other songwriters learn early on that their emotional life is rife with material for new songs, it obviously took Seymour some time for that penny to drop. 'The thing I learned from that record, I realised that anything that's happening to me, anything that's affecting the way I feel, is what I write about, from that album on,' he said. '*Human Frailty* was a point of arrival and a point of departure. It affected everything the band did after that as well.'

which were developed out of relationships, but they weren't directly person-to-person love songs. It was quite a milestone as far as the band was concerned.'

Seymour remembered the song coming during a 'really emotionally switched-on period' in his life, when he was pulling in inspiration from what was happening around him. That was largely a woman called May, who he was in love with. They spent plenty of time in his bedsit over Leo's Spaghetti Bar in St Kilda doing what lovers do, and when she wasn't there he was writing about her.

8 AUSSIE ROCK ANTHEMS

May was also in the other legendary song from *Human Frailty*, 'Say Goodbye'. It wasn't her who uttered the immortal 'You don't make me feel like I'm a woman anymore' line. There are various opinions on where that came from: Seymour said he heard it through the walls while in the manager's office (or in that St Kilda bedsit), while trombone player Waters stated it was he who heard the argument and mentioned it to Seymour. However, the woman grinding her finger into someone's breastbone? Well, that was May.

'I remember coming home from being away touring and going around to see her,' Seymour said. 'She felt that I was taking her for granted. She was sitting on top of me and she's putting her finger in here [on his breastbone], telling me everything but the line "You don't make me feel like I'm a woman any more". I wanted to describe this feeling.'

Back to 'Throw Your Arms Around Me'. Lyrically, the song creates a delicious sense of anticipation. It's not a song about what a lover *is* doing to someone, or *has* done to someone. It's about what they *will* do to them. He will throw his arms around her, he will kiss her in four places (which places they are remain a mystery, but we might be able to guess a few of them), he will shout her name to the blue summer sky. 'I didn't think of it as an unusual device at the time,' Seymour said, 'but in retrospect, you don't hear it that often.'

Despite having a revered status in Australian music history the song was never a hit. When it was released as a single in 1984 the highest point it reached on the charts was No. 38. Instead, the lasting popularity of the song was fuelled by word of mouth, and over time that led to others performing it.

Plenty of artists since have covered the song, either on vinyl or live. The list includes Missy Higgins, Doug Anthony All Stars, Luka Bloom and Katie Noonan, and Crowded House at their farewell gig outside the Sydney Opera House in 1996, but none have surpassed the original. That's in part because the Hunters' version is so good in its simplicity, especially the vocals. Seymour doesn't do a whole lot of emoting or hit any dramatic heights while singing, and the way Seymour sings it is such a crucial part of the song.

THROW YOUR ARMS AROUND ME

Seymour has said that part of the reason the Hunters & Collectors' version works is that he simply plays it straight, letting the natural tone of his voice convey the emotion.

In around 2014 Seymour added a few new verses to the song for live performances in response to a spate of ugly videos posted online in which people verbally abused refugees and migrants:

Oh, whatever world you come from
Yeah, whatever tongue you speak
Well, you can ride my bus any time
I'll stand by you in defeat.

'I found them [the videos] incredibly unnerving so I decided to write this verse about "you can ride my bus any time",' Seymour said. 'I wanted to have that verse in there when we did the Hunters revival in 2014. It felt like a good time to do it, to inspire a sense of community when racism seemed to be becoming a burgeoning political problem. People can take it or leave it. I don't really care whether people like it or not, I just felt like I had to do it.'

Part of the reason 'Throw Your Arms Around Me' makes the No. 1 spot here is to redress a historical oversight. In 1989 triple j launched what became the Hottest 100. For the first three years songs from any year were eligible to be nominated, but the yoof station later changed that to avoid having the same top 10 in different orders every year. In the first two years the song finished at No. 2, losing out to Joy Division's 'Love Will Tear Us Apart'. In the third year it fell to fourth, with Nirvana hogging two of the top three spots. Now, with a No. 1 ranking, an imbalance has been righted.

'Throw Your Arms Around Me' wasn't the only song Hunter & Collectors wrote that became an anthem: another option for this book was their 1992 song 'Holy Grail'. In terms of chart success it did a little better, reaching No. 20. Sporting competitions grabbed onto the song, equating the 'Holy Grail' of the title with whatever cup the teams were fighting for. The Australian Football League in particular loved it so much they used it to plug their finals campaign for several years.

While in hindsight the idea the song might be appropriated for a sporting context isn't all that surprising, 'Holy Grail' has nothing at all to do with footy. It's about the Napoleonic Wars. 'With the lyrics, I'd been reading a Jeanette Winterson novel, *The Passion*,' Seymour remembered. 'It was a story about Napoleon's chef when he invaded Russia. The army was destroyed by the weather. It's a story about survival. It's a really powerful book, and somehow I drew this analogy between the idea of this guy managing to survive this incredible ordeal and Hunters & Collectors making this excruciating record.'

A more odious appropriation happened in 2015 when protest group Reclaim Australia started playing the song at anti-Muslim rallies across the country. Seymour was not impressed with that at all. 'Let me be clear: Reclaim Australia is a racist organisation,' he wrote on Facebook. 'We stand together with refugees and asylum seekers the world over. We are opposed to bigotry, race hate and fascism. Reclaim Australia has no place in Australian society.'

Well said.

THROW YOUR ARMS AROUND ME

CHAPTER 2

Khe Sanh

COLD CHISEL

In 1968 the North Vietnamese Army laid siege to a military base at Khe Sanh. The defenders noticed the North Vietnamese had been moving forces into the area and chose to bolster their own numbers at the base. They added 1000 troops, taking the total to around 6000 at the base, but that was never going to be enough given the enemy was amassing up to 20,000 soldiers.

The siege went on for five long months, with the defenders calling in bombing raids on the enemy. Back home, civilians closely followed news of the defence of Khe Sanh. As is the nature of military commanders, after telling soldiers to stay there and defend the base, in June they changed their minds and decided on an evacuation. The defenders left, taking what they could and destroying the rest so it didn't fall into enemy hands, and were flown out. Ultimately, 274 defenders lost their lives, with 2500 wounded, and thousands of North Vietnamese soldiers were killed. The leaders' orders to hold a base for so long only to decide to suddenly cut and run made those back at home question why they were even in Vietnam in the first place, and whether soldiers were paying too high a price in deaths and casualties. However, it was never an Australian battle: those defenders at Khe Sanh were US Marines commanded by General William Westmoreland, whose strategy was to try and starve the enemy of food and supplies. It didn't work.

That no Australians were there does seem to pose a bit of a problem for Cold Chisel and its songwriter Don Walker. He wrote the song after hearing a musician onstage dedicate a song to this place called Khe Sanh. As writers do, the words caught his attention so he put them in his notebook, until he gradually worked a song around the name – which probably wasn't too hard as the phrase only appears once in the song, in the first line.

At first the historical inaccuracy wasn't anything to worry about, because Walker figured no one would ever see the lyrics. Chisel had been playing it around the traps for a while but had no record deal, and no record deal equals no lyric sheet in an

Walker. 'By that stage it worried me a great deal because I thought I was going to get laughed at, and it would have been justified,' Walker said. 'It didn't happen, [but] it doesn't worry me now. The only important audience in this are veterans, and I know that the song, as far as I have heard, resonates with veterans and I never heard a complaint about the historical inaccuracy of the song.'

One simple solution would have been to change the title to 'Long Tan', an Australian Vietnam war battle. It even has the same number of syllables, meaning it wouldn't seem shoehorned into the first line of the song. It was an idea ex-Redgum singer John Schumann later came up with, though not before he checked with Walker first. 'He rang me up one day a long time ago and asked if I minded if he did that,' Walker remembered. 'I said not only was it absolutely okay with me but "Good on you."'

The song, though it is not as rowdy as much of Cold Chisel's catalogue, has very much become an anthem, sung by suburban cover bands, requested by drunken wags at the back of pubs in Australia, played on FM radio and pushed through stadium speakers at sporting

album . . . and no one seeing Walker's words about a returned Vietnam vet struggling with what we now recognise as post-traumatic stress disorder. 'There was no possibility that anyone would see these lyrics, let alone sing them,' Walker said. 'We were still several years shy of a record contract, and all indications from the Australian music industry were that we would never ever get a record contract or get to make a record.'

Then, finally, someone decided to take a punt on this wild band that every other label had passed on, and suddenly they had a deal. With 'Khe Sanh' recognised as one of the band's more popular songs in their live show, it had to appear on their debut, self-titled album in 1978. That meant people would be able to read the lyrics and hear Jim Barnes's vocals clearly, and the jig would be up for

AUSSIE ROCK ANTHEMS

events. A couple of Walker's mates once texted him from the cricket world cup in London to say it was blaring out at Lords.

Despite or perhaps because of its ubiquity in Australian culture, Walker no longer recognises it as something he wrote. 'If I hear "Khe Sanh" on the radio or if I hear a bunch of people singing it, which I can quite often do anonymously, it never crosses my mind that they're singing my song,' Walker said. 'I don't think about that at all. It's like another entity out there.'

That the five guys in Cold Chisel ever got together is something that suggests the involvement of destiny. While the band formed in Adelaide, only bassist Phil Small hailed from that city. Walker was born in North Queensland and grew up in the New South Wales town of Grafton. Ian Moss came from Alice Springs, Jim Barnes was born in Glasgow and drummer Steve Prestwich grew up in Liverpool. Over time, all five of them ended up in Adelaide as though it was destiny.

The genesis of the band happened when Walker and Moss met up at a jam session where Yes and Pink Floyd were the choice of music. During a break they found a shared preference for the blues. The pair answered an ad placed by bassist Les Kaczmarek to join his band Orange in 1973. The talented Moss was a walk-up starter, but Kaczmarek was a keyboard player so he wasn't sure about Walker – that is, until he heard how the two new guys played together.

KHE SANH 15

Soon after joining Walker had issues with the drummer, so he was replaced with Prestwich via an audition. Their first choice as singer was John Swan, but as he didn't want to play with a bunch of kids he recommended his younger brother Jim. (The different surnames have caused people to think they are step-brothers, but they're not. John kept his father's name when their parents split up, while Jim and his other siblings took on the surname of their mum's new husband.) Barnes joined, but left the band several times before they became big in Australia.

In the early days the band decided the name Orange was a bit crap and changed it to Cold Chisel, the name of an early Walker song. They didn't like that new name much either but figured it would do for the time being, and by the time they thought about changing it again the band was already known around the traps of Sydney. Adopting something else was out of the question, but that was a few years in the future.

In 1973 they were a band interested in playing some originals in a town where everyone played covers. A year later Walker ditched his defence department job, a gig he'd got when he accepted a cadetship while studying maths and physics at uni, for a year's postgraduate study at the University of New England in New South Wales majoring in quantum mechanics. He told the band he'd have no time for playing music, but in an early show of solidarity they packed up and followed him, staying in a farmhouse in the New England town of Kentucky.

The band rehearsed for 10 months while Walker was studying and writing songs on the side. When they got back to Adelaide they presented their new songs to early manager Vince Lovegrove, who felt they were not as good as the covers the band were currently playing. 'He was absolutely right,' Walker remembered. 'No manager in his right mind would have said anything else. The songs were total shit.' Despite having built up a strong following in the tough Adelaide pubs, in 1976 the band decided to try their luck in Melbourne and then Sydney. While the Walker originals didn't go over too well in Adelaide and Melbourne, the tunes worked in Sydney.

As hard as it may be to understand these days, in the late 1970s Cold Chisel struggled mightily to get any interest from record labels. Even Michael Gudinski at independent label Mushroom, the band's preference at the time, wasn't interested – much to his later regret: Cold Chisel turned into quite a cash cow. Normally when a band breaks up sales take a dive, but Chisel's sales kept ticking over during the 1980s, 1990s and beyond. The four compilation albums released in the years between break-up and reformation – *Radio Songs*, *Razor Songs*, *Chisel* and *Teenage Love* – all charted. Only *Razor Songs* missed the top 10, stopping at No. 11, and *Chisel* went platinum an astonishing nine times.

Again, that was all in the future. The only record company that threw Chisel any interest was WEA, but even then some fibbing needed to be done to get the band signed. Chisel had by that time signed up a new manager, Rod Willis, but the WEA execs wanted to end the negotiations because Willis was a newcomer with no management experience. The execs were told that Peter Rix, who was managing the likes of Marcia Hines and Jon English, was Willis's mentor, which got the band over the line. No one told Rix about his involvement with Cold Chisel.

When it came time to record the band's debut self-titled album there were a few hiccups, including that what worked in a live situation didn't work in the studio. For instance, the band sped up through each song. Also, as the band's sole guitarist Moss played both rhythm and lead, chopping and changing as required, but on recordings the guitarist plays rhythm all the way through and the guitar riff and solo are layered on top of that. 'Khe Sanh' aside, many of the songs on that first album were about a woman Walker had been involved with, but they'd split long before the recording. 'Those songs were held over,' he said, 'so they're not that detached. I'm involved there, sometimes to the detriment of the song.'

Once the sessions were finished and the album was mixed, a minor tragedy occurred. The tapes were placed in the boot of a WEA car to be ferried to a local mastering plant,

but for some reason they stayed in the boot for 10 days as the car was driven around in the heat of a Sydney summer. That damaged the quality of the tapes and the eventual mastering made it worse, stripping the oxides off the tape. It was the reason the debut album didn't sound clear and bright, at least not until a proper remix decades later.

When it came out, radio stations wanted a single and the vibe was heavy for 'Khe Sanh'. 'When we started we didn't want to release singles,' Barnes said. 'We wanted to be an albums band like Led Zeppelin. We got talked into releasing "Khe Sanh" as a single by all the radio stations, [which] said: "This song's a hit."' They released it as

KHE SANH 17

a single and watched as it only got scattered airplay everywhere aside from Adelaide. The band was invited to perform the song on the television music program *Countdown*, which would have given it a real boost, but after the rehearsals the ABC's Michael Shrimpton voiced a concern. The line about legs being open but minds being closed was probably not what the kiddies should be hearing on the ABC at 6.00 pm on a Sunday, so could the band change those lines?

It hadn't been the first time this problem cropped up; the band had even recorded an alternate version for the album with the lines 'And their hearts were often open/But their minds were always closed', but it didn't work so the band wiped the take – which had the added benefit of stopping the label from releasing a radio-friendly version.

In the *Countdown* studio the band discussed what to do. The option of agreeing to fudge the original line but then not actually fudging it enough to make it indecipherable was considered but dismissed. Ultimately, the band said 'Thanks, but no thanks' and left the studio. Any attempt to get wider airplay was scotched when the Federation of Radio Broadcasters slapped an A classification on 'Khe Sanh', meaning it couldn't be played on radio at all.

It was another year before radio finally got on board with Cold Chisel, via the pop of 'Choirgirl'. Fortunately most of the people listening to it had no idea what it was about. 'I made a conscious attempt to write a hit single,' Walker said. 'It was a matter of pride and craft. And then I thought, "What'll I write it about?" I wrote it about pregnancy termination and it was a massive hit.'

As for 'Khe Sanh', Barnes remembered when Walker wrote it. He said the keyboard player would be away writing and the band wouldn't hear anything of the songs until he brought in the finished product. 'It might have been in Melbourne and Don walked in and said, "I've got this song. Let's do it

AUSSIE ROCK ANTHEMS

tonight, it's really easy,'" Barnes said. 'And it was really easy for them because there're not many chords, but for me it's like a novel. I had to learn all the words that day. I even said, "I don't know if I can do it," but it's such an engaging lyric that I did it that night.

'The song has held up for three decades because it's a great set of lyrics. It's a really beautiful song and it's as relevant now as it was then. We still have guys going off to fight other people's battles and having to come back and learn how to deal with normal life.' Walker knew several schoolmates from Grafton who had signed up for Vietnam, including one from the next farm over. 'He came back and was severely changed for the worse,' Walker told Debbie Kruger in her book *Songwriters Speak*, 'which was a shame because he was a wonderful bloke.'

Another bloke who went to war was Adelaide guitarist Rick Morris. Walker said one of the important things for him when writing about a situation he'd never experienced was whether there was a ring of truth about it for someone who had been there. 'You're really a long way towards being a bullshit artist if you try [to] write about war experience and you've never been in a war. Rick liked that song. I won't say that it had his seal of approval or anything like that, but he didn't disapprove of it or me for writing it.'

The song has become so legendary that even Australia Post saw fit to recognise it, releasing a 'Khe Sanh' postage stamp in 2001 as part of an Australian rock'n'roll series. Following on from an earlier series released in 1988, this release also included Midnight Oil's 'Power And The Passion', Men at Work's 'Down Under' and John Farnham's 'You're The Voice'. Australia Post gave Chisel another go in 2013 as part of the Australian Legends series, for which those who still wrote letters could lick the back of a stamp honouring the band's *East* album.

Another option for this list was 'Flame Trees', from the band's last studio album before their 1983 break-up. The music was written by Prestwich, who handed it over to Walker to come up with the lyrics. What is often missed in that song is the subtle way Walker looked to slip in an oblique reference to the end of the band, which comes via the use of the phrase 'set fire to this town'. That line is almost identical to one in an earlier song. 'As Cold Chisel was just starting to take off, after we'd been together for a few years, I wrote a song called "Merry-Go-Round" and it's got this phrase in it: "I'm going to set fire to this town,"' Walker said. 'We played that every night as we went from clubs to stadiums and every town around the place both here and overseas.

'"Flame Trees" was a song that was written at the end of our career, pretty much as we were breaking up. Because that phrase had been such a fixture of our live shows I just decided to revisit [it] in a later song. It only appears in two songs, once at the beginning of our ascent and once when the band was in a death dive.'

CHAPTER 3

Beds Are Burning

MIDNIGHT OIL

The band knew they had to try something different. They'd headed to the UK in 1981 to record their album *Place Without A Postcard*, hoping it would be the breakthrough they needed to move them out of the pubs and clubs and up to bigger venues such as entertainment centres. Being in another country saw them cast their eyes back home, and the resulting album was very distinctly Australian. It would please their fanbase but not break new ground, either in their homeland or around the globe.

With pressure building within the band to break through or break up, they went back to London a year later with the intent to shake things up. The result was *10, 9, 8, 7, 6, 5, 4, 3, 2, 1*, an album that saw them move away from their driving Oz-rock pub sound and use electronics, looping and drum machines, despite the initial reluctance of drummer Rob Hirst. It was an album that started with the sound of not guitars and drum, but keyboards and synthesiser effects. That album was huge for Midnight Oil: it went to No. 3 and stayed in the charts for more than three years.

They followed it up with *Red Sails In The Sunset*, a polarising album for fans and one in which the band felt they went too far with the studio trickery. It was recorded around Peter Garrett's run for the Senate on the Nuclear Disarmament Party ticket, which brought with it the very real possibility that had he won, *Red Sails* would be the end of the band.

Still, for all the criticism of *Red Sails* it gave the band their first No. 1 album. In a reaction against the studio-heavy approach, the band's next release was 1985's *Species Deceases*, a four-track EP where the attitude was 'Get in the studio, play the songs and get out.' It enabled the band to blow out the cobwebs and get back to basics.

The desire to strip things right back was taken several steps further with their next album. The band wanted to make a more straightforward album than the last one, *Red Sails In The Sunset*, which they felt had used too much studio effects. Also, unlike the recording process of that album, the band

22   AUSSIE ROCK ANTHEMS

wanted to have the songs written before they entered the studio. For those songs to develop, they needed to go on a trip – one that would change the band forever.

In 1985 the band was approached by the Mutitjulu Aboriginal community, the traditional owners of Uluru, to write a song for a film being made to mark the official return of the monolith to the Aboriginal people. Midnight Oil gave them three songs, and the group chose 'The Dead Heart' over the two other songs: 'You May Not Be Released' and an early version of 'Beds Are Burning'. Songwriters Hirst and Jim Moginie weren't surprised 'Beds Are Burning' was knocked back. 'It was a bit embryonic still,' Moginie said.

'The Dead Heart' was released as a 12-inch single with tracks by First Nations acts Warumpi Band and Coloured Stone on the B-side. One of relatively few songs credited to the whole band, 'The Dead Heart' showed the new direction the band was heading: driven by acoustic guitars and those 'do-de-do-do' harmonies, the song featured space. The song was originally much slower but was sped up on Jim Moginie's advice, and with the help of the producer Nick Launay, sonically the song gave off the vibe of driving along a rutted desert road. It's a subconscious thing, but once you have that in mind it's easy to spot.

BEDS ARE BURNING 23

The song went to No. 4 on the Australian charts and led to an invitation to tour Central Australian First Nation settlements with Warumpi Band. Taking place in the winter of 1986, it forever left its mark on the Sydney band. 'It's as if my life is divided into two halves,' Moginie said. 'The first half is before the Blackfella/Whitefella Tour and the second half is everything after.'

Hirst later described it as 'the most collectively exciting, eye-opening and ultimately saddening experience for us as a band': 'We found people reduced to living under bits of Western refuse, falling prey to Western disease…petrol sniffing, alcoholism

. . . and being misdirected by idiot bureaucrats. But at the same time we were exposed to the positive aspects of Aboriginal culture. There are parts of the trip I still have trouble assimilating years later.'

It also furthered their plan of recording the so-called campfire songs. Early in the tour Midnight Oil played with the same intensity of their Sydney shows, which may have worked in entertainment centres in front of sweaty hordes of fans but on the Northern Territory's red sands under the night sky it was overkill. The band quickly realised that when the locals kept their distance from the stage. 'I think it took us a while to change things,' Moginie said, 'to get into the slower pace, but it wasn't planned or even discussed. It made things more musical, more hypnotic .. . If you play more quietly, you draw people in closer to hear. We learnt a bit of seduction.'

'Beds Are Burning' was played on that tour. A documentary filmed at the time shows a version still in development, at a slower tempo and with different lyrics. Hirst told Kruger the title came from an art exhibition he'd seen in the Sydney suburb of Paddington. 'It related to the impact of Mussolini's Fascists upon the lives of

AUSSIE ROCK ANTHEMS

ordinary Italians: "How can we sleep when our beds are burning?"'

Once the band returned to Sydney, songs that ended up on 1987's *Diesel And Dust* album started coming out. Moginie wrote 'Warakurna', while Hirst came up with 'Bullroarer' as well as others such as 'Sell My Soul' and 'Sometimes'. 'Beds Are Burning' started to take shape, the lyrics name-checking some of the places they had visited on the legendary tour – places such as Kintore and Yuendemu. Garrett got a songwriting credit for what was the most confronting part for many white Australians.

BEDS ARE BURNING

Garrett decided a statement needed to be made and offered up the phrase 'Let's give it back', which Hirst ended up using as a bridge in the song. It nailed the Oils' colours to the mast and made it absolutely clear where they stood with the issue.

Today, lines such as 'It belongs to them/ Let's give it back' and 'The time has come to say fair's fair/ To pay the rent, to pay our share' don't make people uncomfortable, but it was a different world in 1987 when the song was released. The groundbreaking Mabo decision that overturned the long-held idea of terra nullius was five years away, as was then–Prime Minister Paul Keating's legendary Redfern Speech. When 'Beds Are Burning' came out the idea of land rights, of handing back land, wasn't on most Australians' radar.

The band knew the message could be divisive. 'There was a sense of helplessness about the issue at the time,' Moginie said. 'It felt like screaming into a fog of indifference. When the album was ready to be released we were prepared to be shouted down by every closet racist in the country. The issue of Aboriginal dispossession had been effectively ignored up to that point. Aboriginals only got the vote in the 1960s and a lot of the information about stolen children hadn't yet come to light.'

Those concerns didn't stop the success of 'Beds Are Burning' or the *Diesel And Dust* album. The former reached No. 6 in Australia, while the latter went all the way to No. 1. It could even be said the song gave people something to think about and helped to break down a few barriers. More surprisingly, what was a song and album with a distinctly Australian flavour found success overseas, especially given the lack of response to the Australian focus of their earlier *Place Without A Postcard* album. 'I've always had this dream that this band could write Australian music that people overseas could get on to and understand,' Hirst said, 'and which would enlarge their whole vision of Australia past Vegemite sandwiches and kangaroo hops.'

That dream came true. 'Beds Are Burning' went top 10 in countries around the world, pulling *Diesel And Dust* along with it. It saw the band punch its way into the coveted US market, with the single going into the top 20 while the album reached No. 21. The band had

tried to crack the US market with *10, 9, 8, 7, 6, 5, 4, 3, 2, 1* and *Red Sails In The Sunset*, but sales weren't strong enough to get the attention and promotion of their record company.

What helped 'Beds Are Burning' was the fallout from the payola scandal in the United States. For years labels had hired promoters – at arm's length – to press radio programmers to play their songs. When news broke about Mafia links to the promoters everyone scrambled to put as much distance between themselves and the payola process, which led to radio picking songs on merit rather than payoffs. That played right into Midnight Oil's hands.

'So what happened was the radio stations all decided to pick "Beds Are Burning" by "this Aussie band Midnight Oil", just to prove that they were not under the influence of payola,' band manager Gary Morris told Midnight Oil biographer Mark Dodshon. 'They started playing "Beds" right across America, and as a result it started to convert to record sales and "Beds Are Burning" became a hit in America. As a result of being a top-10 hit in America it converted to Europe and then went around the planet.'

The band enjoyed a few years of success in the US, with the follow-up 1990 *Blue Sky Mining* album going gold, but the band

eventually got worn out by the seemingly never-ending American tours. It's a big place, and to capitalise on the momentum Midnight Oil had built up they needed to be there for months at a time. They weren't keen on that, and to the surprise of their US label the band took an extended break. 'We just needed to defuse,' Hirst said. 'I mean, how could it be any other way? You've got people in intense situations and circumstances, all living in each other's pockets for months at a time. Of course you're going to be at each other's throats unless you have time off.'

Nothing was going to tempt them to cut short their break, not even an invitation from MTV to play on their New Year's Eve show – an offer other bands would kill for. But Midnight Oil didn't care. They always looked to go their own way, even if it was the wrong way to so many others. That contrary nature showed up on their next album *Earth And Sun And Moon*, which was released three

years after *Blue Sky Mining*. Having had enough of the almost mainstream stylings of the sound that made them in the US, the band recorded a more laid-back album right when the guitar-heavy grunge sound was the flavour of the month.

Sure, the record company wasn't exactly chuffed, but as we know Midnight Oil just didn't care. ✸

BEDS ARE BURNING

CHAPTER 4

It's A Long Way To The Top
(If You Wanna Rock'n'Roll)

AC/DC

Bon Scott was the legendary frontman at the microphone for this hit, as well as many others from AC/DC's heyday, but he wasn't the singer on the band's first-ever vinyl release. That honour went to the band's previous singer Dave Evans, whose vocal chords you can hear on the 1974 debut 'Can I Sit Next To You, Girl'. Well, you would be able to hear them if you could manage to locate a copy.

In the world of AC/DC recordings that debut has very much slipped through the cracks and the band, which preferred everyone think their recording career began with Scott, would have liked it to stay that way. Copies have been known to hit prices of $2000 or more; it's quite the collector's item.

If you don't want to hear it direct from the vinyl, there is a video for the song floating around online – and the band *definitely* would prefer you didn't see it. It catches AC/DC in their very short glam phase, which was the idea of Malcolm Young, who later tried to sheet the blame home to Evans. They definitely do not look like the Acca Dacca you're used to and especially not Malcolm Young, who is wearing black pants with knee-high boots, a black and yellow striped top with puffy sleeves and a matching tam-o'-shanter. He's the most ridiculously dressed person onstage, so much so that you barely notice brother Angus in his school uniform get-up.

The song itself is very poppy, sounding more like Slade than AC/DC. Perhaps in an attempt to erase Evans's presence the band re-recorded 'Can I Sit Next To You, Girl' not long after Scott joined for the band's second album *TNT*, and it found its way to the B-side of 'It's A Long Way To The Top'. For the second go-round they knocked off some of the glam edges – though not all of them – to bring it into line with the now-accepted AC/DC sound.

If the Young family never took advantage of Australia's assisted migration scheme in 1963, our music scene would have been so much the poorer. In June 1963, after putting up with a freezing cold snap that seemed to last forever, the Young clan decided to leave the postwar Glasgow housing estate of Cranhill for Australia.

If a family ends up with one famous musician among their brood that's special enough, but the Youngs ended up with three. George Young was first, forming one of Australia's first internationally successful acts, The Easybeats. After that band ran out of puff he and Easybeats guitarist Harry Vanda created a powerful songwriting and producing duo known as Vanda and Young. Together, they left their fingerprints all over the Australian music scene in the 1970s, creating hits for the likes of Easybeats frontman Stevie Wright, John Paul Young and others while also taking charge of the Alberts label, where they brought in bands such as The Angels and Rose Tattoo.

That sort of CV would be impressive for any family but younger brothers Malcolm and Angus followed in George's footsteps, creating AC/DC, which went on to achieve worldwide fame and is still recording and performing music an unbelievable five decades later.

Obviously big brother George would be a guiding light for the band in the

early days. Having been through the music industry wringer himself, he had plenty of advice to pass on. Perhaps the most lasting stemmed from The Easybeats' efforts to find a follow-up to the international hit 'Friday On My Mind'. They made their way down odd musical alleys that led nowhere instead of sticking with what they were good at and then letting the market come to them. That advice AC/DC followed to a tee, leading many to joke the band simply released the same album over and over again. Also, the fact that Malcolm and Angus saw that their older brother had made it overseas, albeit briefly, meant international success was viewed as a realistic possibility.

Malcolm Young had been playing in a few bands since leaving school, including The Velvet Underground – not *that* one, a different one. Angus, meanwhile, was doing his thing in Kantuckee, a band reputedly named for Angus's love of a new restaurant called Kentucky Fried Chicken that had just arrived in Australia. In November 1973 the two brothers ended up in the same band, though for the sake of band harmony Malcolm made Angus audition first. It was the last time the brothers put other band members ahead of themselves.

The following year Malcolm came up with the idea of putting his brother in a school uniform. According to original singer Dave Evans, the dress-ups didn't stop there. 'Malcolm said, "I'm going to wear like an airman's outfit, like a satin airman's outfit with boots," a jumpsuit-type thing. He wanted the three other boys to think of something, so the drummer at the time came up with the top hat and the harlequin outfit and the bass player had the idea to look like a New York cop with a crash helmet, jodhpurs and dark glasses. I went for the Slade bottom half with the tights and platform boots and a top half like Rod Stewart, with a striped jacket and scarf.'

That look didn't last long for AC/DC, and neither did most of the band members. In the early days only Malcolm and Angus stayed in the band, with drummers and bassists regularly punted and replaced. In late 1974 the biggest of those changes took place: it was Evans' turn to be sacked, because a singer named Bon Scott had caught the attention of the Young brothers after an audition.

Scott had experienced a certain level of pop stardom in Adelaide band The Valentines, which had a minor hit with the not very good 'My Old Man's A Groovy Old Man'. Scott had also gigged for a while as singer for blues hippie band Fraternity. In May 1974 he jumped on his motorbike angry and drunk and rode it into a car. He spent two weeks in hospital wondering if his shot at being a star had come and gone.

Scott was staring his 30s in the face, meaning he was well past the age when a musician was supposed to have made it. That age gap alone – the Youngs were barely out of their teens in 1974 – made the idea of Scott joining AC/DC seem far-fetched. The Youngs couldn't see how this broken-down old hippie could be the lead singer they were looking for, but they gave him a try after Valentines member Vince Lovegrove raved about Scott to George Young.

The day after Scott saw them play a show he turned up to a jam session with the Youngs and a few other musicians, though only Scott and the Youngs knew this was an audition. They'd even downplayed the whole thing to Evans so that he didn't turn up. The brothers jammed with Scott for hours and then, after a brief confab, they offered the old hippie the job. Rather than jumping at the chance he mulled it over for a few weeks before accepting a call for help, and the job, after Evans kept calling in sick.

From that moment things moved fast: six weeks after joining Scott was in the studio working on AC/DC's first album. Called *High Voltage*, it was the sound of a band still trying to work out their identity.

It didn't help that there was a revolving door attitude to their rhythm section. *High Voltage* was released in February 1975 and reached a respectable No. 14 on the charts. A month after that release they were back in the studio working on a follow-up, and this time the result was much stronger – no doubt aided by the fact they'd finally settled on a rhythm section in bassist Mark Evans and drummer Phil Rudd. The second album, *TNT*, was released in time for Christmas and went to No. 2. It also spawned a trio of iconic AC/DC songs in 'It's A Long Way To The Top', 'TNT' and 'High Voltage'.

In a move that has confused people for decades, the US market chose not to release these two albums. Instead, they picked the eyes out of them to make a compilation, supporting the view that the debut album wasn't that great: seven of the nine songs came from *TNT*. Problem was, the US label in their wisdom chose to call this compilation *High Voltage*, meaning AC/DC would forever have two different albums of that title in their discography. Over time the US version of *High Voltage* officially became the 'only' version, and when the band released a box set of its albums that version was the one that appeared. To be fair, the band itself also confused things because the song 'High Voltage' wasn't on the album of that name but rather on its *TNT* follow-up.

This wasn't the only time the US market tinkered with AC/DC records. In 1976 US label Atlantic said 'No' to *Dirty Deeds Done Dirt Cheap*. After the huge success of *Back In Black*, Atlantic decided to cash in and finally released *Dirty Deeds*, in an album sleeve that looked like something from a 1990s pop-punk band.

IT'S A LONG WAY TO THE TOP

momentum of the band following the mega-selling *Back In Black*. They even took 'Jailbreak', perhaps the best song on the album, off the US version. That song finally saw the light of day on an EP in 1984, along with bits and pieces from their first two Australian albums.

Anyway, back to the Australian *TNT* album. It opened with the legendary track 'It's A Long Way To The Top', which was also the first single from the album. It was truly AC/DC's first classic song. The first time George heard his brothers play it he didn't like it. The brothers had over-rehearsed the song, making it too polished, so they were told to play it live until they figured out how the song worked – and that's what they did, coming back to George with a much tighter, harder version. The lyrics

Plenty of new AC/DC fans who had been listening to Brian Johnson singing on *Back In Black* were confronted with the band's next release featuring a completely different singer. 'Releasing *Dirty Deeds* was one of the most crass decisions ever made by a record company executive,' Phil Carson, the man who signed the band to Atlantic, said. He felt the *Dirty Deeds* decision arrested the

came from Scott, who was writing from experience about the hard road of being in a band. It was his CV set to music.

The standout in the song, the thing that makes you prick up your ears, is the inclusion of the bagpipes: a most un–rock'n'roll instrument. To give the song a point of difference by bringing in the bagpipes was George's idea, and he was further swayed by

36 AUSSIE ROCK ANTHEMS

Scott saying he had played in a Scottish pipe band back in Fremantle.

Someone headed down the road to a music store and paid $435, which would have bought two electric guitars back then, for a set of bagpipes. Bassist Evans got a good laugh out of watching the three Scotsmen in his band and their brother George struggle to put together the bagpipes. It was then that Scott came clean: yes, he had really played in a pipe band, but he had been the drummer. Still, he managed to wrangle a few sounds out of the bagpipes, perhaps helped by playing the recorder in his younger years.

However, Scott didn't do it without the help of some studio trickery. George Young had Malcolm, Rudd and Evans blow the drones, which were the big pipes sticking out of the top of the bag that created the constant harmonising drone heard when the bagpipes played. That was sampled by George Young and built into a tape loop that Scott later added to when he played his bit on the chanter, the recorder-like bit that sticks out of the bottom of the bag.

While it was the first of a number of classic rock songs AC/DC released during their creative high point in the 1970s, 'It's A Long Way To The Top' just squeaked into the top 10 at No. 9. The song might have a long way to go to No. 1, but the chart position was no doubt helped by the video shot by *Countdown* in February 1976. Usually a band has to pay to make their own videos, but here was a TV show willing to make one for them – and one that everyone remembers now when they hear the song.

The video shows the band playing on the back of a flatbed truck driving down Swanston Street in Melbourne. Malcolm Young claimed he had had the idea for ages, but it's likely he was inspired more recently than that: in 1975 The Rolling Stones drove down Fifth Avenue in New York to promote their US tour. *Countdown* producer Paul Drane recalled the truck had to make four passes along Swanston Street to get enough footage for the video. That was a logistical effort itself, because it meant the truck had to find space to turn around before heading back down the street again. There was also the safety factor: even though the truck was travelling very slowly, it wasn't easy for the band to maintain their

IT'S A LONG WAY TO THE TOP 37

balance. 'A few times a few of us nearly came off the truck,' Angus Young said. 'It was a case of, you know, Bon would go "I'll hold the back of your shorts" and Malcolm would lean against Bon.'

Despite 'It's A Long Way To The Top' being a legendary song, AC/DC rarely played it live. Since Scott's passing Brian Johnson won't touch it out of respect, because it was Bon's signature song. That leaves the period between the song's release in 1976 and Scott's death in February 1980 as the only time the song might have been played live. Part of the problem with playing the song live was those damned bagpipes. It was hard to get them and the guitars in tune with each other, and during the stage show Scott didn't have the breath to power the bagpipes – and that was even when the band was playing live to a recording of the bagpipe drone, to which Scott would play a few notes over the top.

Some estimates have the number of times 'Long Way' was played live as just over 200, but former bassist Mark Evans thought that was overstating things. 'If we played it maybe 60, 70 times live that would be it,' he said. 'Someone sent me a bootleg of us playing it at Hobart Town Hall and it was like listening to another song.

'We didn't play it a lot and I think it had a lot to do with the bagpipes. In time it became iconic and associated with the band, but oddly enough the band doesn't play it. It has become a lot bigger song than when it first came out. [Then] it was relatively successful for us as a single in Australia, but "Jailbreak", "High Voltage" and "TNT" were certainly a lot bigger.'

The last time the bagpipes appeared on stage for this song is believed to be a concert at St Albans High School in Victoria on 3 March 1976. In footage of the show, towards the end of 'It's A Long Way To The Top' Scott heads over to stage left and drops the bagpipes at the edge of the stage – or, at least, he tries to. Before the pipes hit the floor the crowd drag them away and likely tore them to pieces in the quest for a souvenir.

CHAPTER 5

Working Class Man

JIMMY BARNES

This guy named Jimmy Barnes didn't exist before 1986. Before then, the frontman of Cold Chisel was always credited on albums as 'Jim Barnes'. 'Jimmy' was born only after that band's demise, likely because everyone had been calling him Jimmy anyway so why not make it official? Whether Jim or Jimmy, he was partially responsible for the demise of Cold Chisel.

In the early days of the band Don Walker was the driving force behind Cold Chisel. Older than the rest of his band members, he led the way and the others followed and it was largely his songs that powered the band. However, by the early 1980s the band members had developed lives outside Cold Chisel and were themselves contributing songs to the band as well. Also, a breakthrough into markets outside Australia had proven elusive. A US tour didn't go well, and at a 1983 set of dates in Germany the band played so badly Walker kicked over his keyboard and stormed offstage.

The tensions within the band led to the decision to sack drummer Steve Prestwich, hoping it might fix something. Instead, it hastened the end, the band realising that simply hiring a new drummer wasn't going to solve the problem. The final straw came when Barnes asked for a $30,000 advance, although in his authorised biography he said he asked for $5000. Under the partnership arrangement that governed the band, if one member got $30,000 then the other members had to get that amount as well. An outgoing of $150,000 would clean out the band's bank balance, so the other members said 'No.'

Barnes called a band meeting. 'They just thought it was me bullshitting as usual, talking heated,' Barnes said. 'I'd thought about it and I tried to explain that things weren't right. I said, "I've got to go" and they decided not to go on. After it was decided that the band would not continue, we agreed to announce it as though it was a group decision and [we also made] a conscious decision not to let people know, because we weren't going to air our dirty

laundry.' The band announced a farewell tour called the Last Stand and worked on their last album, *Twentieth Century*. It album came out in April 1984, four months after Cold Chisel had disbanded.

Mushroom Records boss Michael Gudinski, who had famously passed on Cold Chisel in the mid-1970s, started chasing Barnes's signature. Back in the mid-1970s, two Adelaide bands had been presented to him: Chisel and Stars. He chose poorly, signing Stars, and losing a great big cash cow in Cold Chisel. As well as releasing the albums he could have signed up Don Walker's publishing and taken on management of the band among other likely revenue streams. The band were keen to sign with Mushroom, but Gudinski passed.

With Barnes now looking to become a solo performer, Gudinski wanted him at Mushroom. 'Jimmy loves reminding me that I had the chance to sign Cold Chisel, but I'm adamant that Jimmy wasn't singing on the demos that I heard,' Gudinski said. 'Whatever happened, there was no way I was going to miss out on signing Jimmy when he went solo.' Gudinski had the advantage that he and Barnes had become friends, and soon enough the former Cold Chisel frontman signed with Mushroom.

Barnes wasted no time in launching his solo career, rounding up a backing band less than a month after the Chisel split. That line-up included Ray Arnott, who had drummed for Chisel on their last album, Bruce Howe from Fraternity, with whom Barnes had sung in Chisel's early days, and long-time pub rock guitarist Mal Eastick. His first solo single, 'No Second Prize', came out in August 1984. Written by Barnes in 1980, it was demoed by Cold Chisel but never released. Like the tune 'Letter To Alan' from the band's *Circus Animals* album, 'No Second Prize' was a tribute to Chisel roadies Alan Dallow and Billy Rowe, who died in a truck crash in 1980.

During the recording Barnes decided to put the wind up his new label boss. He rang Gudinski raving about the new material the band was recording and how he had to come up and hear it. 'I flew to Sydney and Jimmy played me five new songs, five hokey, corny, terrible country songs,' Gudinski remembered. 'He was buzzing, "What do

WORKING CLASS MAN

you think? What do you think?" He could see the colour draining from my face. "I'll have to think about it," I replied. "I'm not quite sure."

'Jimmy handed me the cassette: it was labelled "Jim's Barn Band". I'd been had.'

Barnes' real solo debut went to No. 12 and he followed it up with his first album *Bodyswerve*, named for a soccer move and also for Barnes and wife Jane's habit of sending friends off to a party and then heading off in a different direction, in September. It shot to No. 1 and spawned a second single, 'Daylight', also a tune demoed by Chisel back in the day. His signature tune, however, came from another songwriter.

His record label saw Barnes's follow-up album as a chance to break into the US market and hooked him up with a number of American songwriters for some of the tracks. Barnes spent three months in the United States in 1985 shuffling around from one songwriter to the next. 'I spent months and months in LA and San Francisco writing and meeting people,' he told biographer Toby Creswell. 'At one point I was writing with three or four different songwriters a day. One minute you'd be writing this strange dirty Dylanesque song and then, next minute, you're writing a Madonna song.'

Ultimately, Barnes picked the songwriters he had some chemistry with and spent more time with them. One of those, Jonathan Cain of arena rock act Journey, wrote the

44 AUSSIE ROCK ANTHEMS

song that changed Barnes's life. It was initially put forward as a ballad until Barnes decided to rough it up. 'Jonathan's impression after meeting me and listening to my record was that my audience was working class, honest and straightforward, and he hit the nail right on the head. Soon after he rang me up and said, "I've got a song for you." I went back to see him and he played me "Working Class Man". From the moment I heard it I knew it was great. I recorded it, but I had to go back to Australia to do a Tasmanian tour. Jonathan mixed the song and sent it to me.'

The relationship with Barnes and Cain wasn't as smooth as the Australian singer made out. At one stage Gudinski had to fly to the US to smooth over tensions between the pair. The combination of Barnes's hot-headedness and Cain's tendency to see himself as the real talent made for a volatile situation. It got worse when, according to Stuart Coupe's biography on Gudinski, 'Working Class Man' later turned up in an Australian ad for Mazda. Cain's publisher had done the deal – after all, it was his song – but the American didn't bother to give Barnes any advance warning.

The lyrics of the song clearly show Cain's American bent, with references to God and Elvis, serving in Vietnam and being mad at Uncle Sam (the album track 'American Heartbeat' was more obvious), not that it made any difference to Barnes's Australian audience. The tune became *the* Jimmy Barnes song, resulting in him being forever after called the working-class man despite the fact that Barnes insisted the song wasn't about him at all. 'Most people thought it was

WORKING CLASS MAN   45

The flames were a problem in the cane fields too. During Queensland tours he'd seen the old practice of burning cane fields and viewed the video shoot as his chance to see what happened up close . . . Perhaps a little too close. In the climax to the video when Barnes mimes the song in front of the flames you can see him look nervously over his shoulder to see how close the fire is. 'As it burned it created a whirlpool of fire, and it wasn't long until I was in the middle of it,' Barnes told the ABC. 'I thought I was about to go up in flames along with the cane.'

written about me, but it was actually written about my audience: staunch honest people who work and who care. I perform it as a tribute to them,' he said.

The video for the song was shot in the Port Kembla steelworks and the cane fields of North Queensland at a time when occupational health and safety apparently wasn't an issue. There Barnes is at the steelworks, standing in front of a huge cauldron of fire wearing a sleeveless T-shirt and no hard hat. Had any of those sparks landed on Barnes' cotton T-shirt it would have gone up in flames.

Cane farmer Johnny Jashar remembered someone running to the house to get a large bucket of water to pour over an overheating Barnes. The farmer had no idea he was being filmed for what became a legendary music video. 'My boss had said "Comb your hair tomorrow because the cameras will be there" but didn't explain much more,' Jashar said. 'I thought it was a television ad for the new tractors we were driving. I didn't know who Jimmy Barnes was.'

The accompanying album *For The Working Class Man* was a strange beast indeed. Its 12 tracks were spread out across two vinyl albums, and side two of the first disc only had two songs on it and a run time of less than eight minutes. On top of that, it seemed Barnes was double-dipping: there were only five new songs on the album, the seven remaining tracks being remixed versions from the *Bodyswerve* album. Conscious that the 100,000 fans who bought the first album might baulk at paying full price for another record full of the same songs, Barnes struck a deal with his Australian label Mushroom. The first 100,000 copies of *For The Working Class Man* were sold at $9.99 rather than the planned $13.99. The ploy worked, with the album going to No. 1 on the Australian charts and ultimately going platinum seven times. Oddly, the 'Working Class Man' single climbed no higher than No. 5 – yes, Barnes's iconic song never made it to No. 1.

Barnes got a lot of mileage out of the song: his autobiography of a traumatic childhood was named *Working Class Boy* and the follow-up was called *Working Class Man*. He also turned both into movies and live shows. There's no doubt the idea of Barnes being working class has served him very well, and it also saw others try to ride in his slipstream in the hope some of Barnes's credibility would rub off on them. One of those was former federal treasurer Josh Frydenberg, who visited the Port Kembla steelworks along with Prime Minister Malcolm Turnbull and decided to invoke the image of Barnesy.

WORKING CLASS MAN

'More than 30 years ago Jimmy Barnes came to Port Kembla to make the film clip for "Working Class Man",' Frydenberg said. 'Well, today the prime minister has come to Port Kembla to create jobs for working-class men and women.'

Barnes quickly slapped down the treasurer via Twitter. 'Hey Josh Frydenberg don't use my name or my songs to sell your shitty policies. You don't represent me,' Barnes wrote. He also had to step in when racist groups such as Reclaim Australia used his songs during protests in 2015.

'It has come to my attention that certain groups of people have been using my voice, my songs as their anthems at

rallies,' he wrote on Facebook. 'I only want to say the Australia I belong to and love is a tolerant Australia. A place that is open and giving. It is a place that embraces all sorts of different people, in fact it is made stronger by the diversity of its people. If you look at my family you can see we are a multicultural family. Australia needs to stand up for love and tolerance in these modern times. None of these people represent me and I do not support them.'

One person who was able to use 'Working Class Man' without any blowback was comedian Adam Hills. The performer had a routine where he sung the national anthem 'Advance Australia Fair' to various other tunes. At the 1997 Edinburgh Comedy Festival he sang it to the tune of TV show themes for *Gilligan's Island* and *The Beverly Hillbillies*. Hills said it got to the stage where he would hear a song and automatically think 'Will the anthem fit into this?'

One of those happened to be a certain song by Jimmy Barnes. 'One day I was in a shopping centre and "Working Class Man" was on the speaker system, and I thought, "Wow, wouldn't it be great if the national anthem fits to this?"' Hills said. 'So I started trying it out, and to my surprise not only did it fit but it fit really well and the rest is history.'

Barnes saw Hills's effort when he was a guest on music quiz show *Spicks and Specks*, and reportedly gave it his approval.

CHAPTER 6

I Touch Myself

DIVINYLS

As hard as it might be to believe, there is a link between the rough-edged rock of Divinyls and Australian yacht rockers Air Supply. The latter band was founded when Russell Hitchcock and Graham Russell met in 1975 while working on the musical *Jesus Christ Superstar*. They were joined by bassist Jeremy Paul and, on guitar, a guy named Mark McEntee.

That was the line-up that recorded Air Supply's 1976 self-titled debut, which included the hit 'Love And Other Bruises'. Soon after the release of the album McEntee left to become a session musician, but by the end of the 1970s he'd decided he wanted to form his own band – and he didn't want it to sound anything like Air Supply. 'I wanted to do a rock band,' he told Double J. 'I had all these musical ideas and stuff and I didn't want to do a normal band at that time. I wanted it to be a proper rock band. A lot of people were playing that disco music at that stage. They were doing mild stuff and I didn't want to do mild stuff, I didn't want to do polite music.'

McEntee and Paul formed the Divinyls, with the latter introducing the former to firebrand singer Chrissy Amphlett when she was singing in a choir.

Amphlett came with a very colourful history. The cousin of Patricia Amphlett, who had had success in the 1960s as Little Pattie, she was just 21 but had been singing since she was aged 14. She'd packed up and left Australia for several years, living on the streets of Paris and spending three months in a Spanish prison for illegal busking and dope smoking, both of which the authorities took a dim view of. (While in Divinyls, Amphlett spent time in jail over parking fines, opting to wipe the debt that way rather than just paying the fines.) She remembered spending her time behind those Spanish bars drawing portraits of other prisoners to keep on their good side, and also the coffee, which was so bad she used to throw it up.

When she was 17 Amphlett played the role of Linda Lips the Porn Queen in the Australian version of the R-rated musical *Let My People Come*, where she got to sing

52 AUSSIE ROCK ANTHEMS ★ ★ ★ ★ ★ ★

a song called 'Give It To Me' and was the understudy for another character with the song, ahem, 'Come In My Mouth'. *Let My People Come* was famous, or infamous, because the singers and actors at one point in the show performed in the nude,' Amphlett wrote in her autobiography.

McEntee found that he and Amphlett gelled very quickly, especially in terms of songwriting. 'I would get an idea for a song,' he said, 'and she would, more or less, have a similar idea. So it used to work out without too much trying to graft anything or work on anything.' They were also on the same page when it came to creating music that was still rough around the edges. 'Chrissy cottoned on to that and knew that together we could create that. We didn't want to make musical mistakes, but we wanted to do it without sounding like anyone else. We wanted to sound different.'

The Divinyls started honing their chops in 1981, in the Sydney pub-rock scene. Midnight Oil drummer Rob Hirst remembered that scene as a testing time for many bands: in front of wild crowds, you either hardened up or went home. 'Men with their shirts off, fighting, throwing beer around, vomiting on each other's shoes, it was just visceral,' Hirst said. 'The kind of music that you had to make was like that. That's why The Angels made the kind of music they made, that's why we had to toughen up from our prog-surfie roots. Long story short, the Divinyls could also do that, a fantastic live band.'

For Hirst, it was a band led by the best female rock singer Australia has ever produced. 'She went into a zone that no one

else could come close to,' he said. 'There was no vanity there. She just let rip.'

McEntee agreed that the Sydney pub scene gave the band the chance to develop quickly, in part because they got to play so often. 'Everyone would go out to the pubs to see bands play. Bands would get really good at live performances, because they'd be playing to people all the time. They'd learn how to work a crowd. In the world scene Australia was kind of unique in those days.'

Having a female singer out front also helped the band stand out, especially one that was clearly *part* of the band and not just an add-on. 'Before Chrissy Amphlett and the Divinyls, rarely did a female performer front a band,' cousin Patricia said. 'And if they did, they weren't actually *fronting* the band. But when Chrissy came along it was like "Move over, you fellas, it's all about me now." She broke the mould of the very male-dominated world of rock music. She broke that forever.'

The wild, 'don't give a fuck' image took a while for Amphlett to create. Manager Vince Lovegrove remembered she would stand at the back of the stage and sing while staring at the floor. 'Up on stage I was no more animated than a statue,' she said. The solution was the old performance trick of creating a character who would take the stage each night, someone who was different from the offstage Chrissy Amphlett. 'I needed something I could hide behind that would free me to let loose,' she said.

That camouflage was the school tunic, an idea in part borrowed from AC/DC's Angus Young and his schoolboy image. Amphlett combined that with a haircut that partly covered her eyes, allowing her to not 'see' the audience, and a character she variously called 'The Monster' or 'The Schoolgirl' – turning the schoolgirl fantasy held by many of the men in the crowd on its ear. 'Being The Schoolgirl gave me a freedom I'd never known. I owned that stage, and the audience in front of it. I could dance madly and charge furiously back and forth across the stage. I could dive into the crowd. I could scowl and yell and swear at the audience and no one dared answer back.'

The band's big break came via film director Ken Cameron. Already a fan of the band, he wanted to use their music in his new movie *Monkey Grip*, based on Helen Garner's book of the same name about a single mother living in Melbourne sharehouses and in love with a flaky heroin addict. The band's first release would be an EP of the movie's soundtrack.

'It was really great,' McEntee said, 'because through doing that we recorded all that stuff at Albert studios. Ken wanted to use "Girlfriends", "Boys In Town", "Only Lonely" [and] "Elsie", so funnily enough he chose these songs we already had.' It also meant they got to make a cheap video for their debut single 'Boys In Town': 'We did something whereby we would get our film clip filmed as well, because it was part of

I TOUCH MYSELF 55

the movie,' McEntee said. 'That was a great clip, that first "Boys In Town" clip with that microphone. The neon tube, I'd never seen that done before! And I think it was the camera guy's idea, I can't remember. We were lucky, we had a lot of facilities that were there for that film that we got to use.'

'Boys In Town' was a killer debut for the band, reaching No. 8 on the charts, though many may have missed the feminist subtext in the lyrics. It's about a woman who had been sleeping around with all the boys in town as a way of trying to fit in, but decided to push them away because she'd realised how foolish she was and how little they respected her. Amphlett admitted the content made it a difficult song to sing onstage, although the introduction of the schoolgirl outfit changed all that. It allowed Amphlett to take on a character and have that character – rather than herself – be the person who was the subject of the lyrics to songs such as 'Boys In Town'.

The band's debut full-length album, *Desperate*, came out in 1983. Boasting 'Boys In Town' and another Divinyls classic, 'Science Fiction', the album went to No. 5 on the charts. The sudden rise led to rampant drug and alcohol use in the band, which resulted in rising tensions and increasing gaps between albums. *What A Life!* came out two years after their debut and the third album, *Temperamental*, three years after that.

They had been chasing overseas success, especially in the US, but to no avail. However, that changed with the 1991 release of a self-titled album annoyingly stylised as *diVINYLS*, although by this time the band was really only McEntee and Amphlett. That was the album that included the single 'I Touch Myself', which gave the band its only No. 1 Australian single but also went to No. 4 in the US and top 10 in the UK.

The song was the outcome of an unusual four-way songwriting partnership between Amphlett and McEntee and Americans Billy Steinberg and Tom Kelly. Steinberg and Kelly already had runs on the board when it came to songwriting, having penned Madonna's 'Like A Virgin', 'Eternal Flame' for The Bangles, 'True Colours' for Cyndi Lauper and 'So Emotional' for Whitney Houston, all of which were No. 1 songs.

AUSSIE ROCK ANTHEMS

I TOUCH MYSELF

Steinberg met Amphlett at the Cat & Fiddle restaurant on Sunset Boulevard in Hollywood. He had brought along his notebook of ideas, which featured song titles and partially completed lyrics. 'I wanted to see which ones she responded to,' Steinberg said, 'so I nervously pulled out my notebook and allowed her to look through these lyrics. I say "nervously" because I feel really nervous and self-conscious when someone's reading my notebooks.' In that notebook was just the first verse and chorus of a song called 'I Touch Myself'. Amphlett gravitated to the song, partially because of the idea of a sexually explicit song being played on the radio. Her selection pleased Steinberg, because that was his favourite from the notebook as well.

The following day they met up with Kelly and McEntee to work on the music and the rest of the words. Despite the explicit nature of the song, Amphlett said she didn't feel awkward writing them with virtual strangers. 'It was just fun,' she told Kruger, 'being silly and having fun.'

In Australia the song did everyone a favour, knocking Vanilla Ice's 'Ice Ice Baby' out of the No. 1 spot. It also charted around the world, helped by a music video from future blockbuster movie director Michael Bay. That such a song became a hit and got airplay despite the subject matter shouldn't really come as too much of a surprise. After all, there are so many hit songs that are solely about sex. In 1976 Starland Vocal Band had a hit with 'Afternoon Delight', though the

AUSSIE ROCK ANTHEMS

song is about not waiting for the sun to go down to hook up. Cyndi Lauper went to No. 3 in 1984 with 'She Bop', a song about masturbation; even a cursory look at the lyrics would make that obvious.

With 'I Touch Myself' there was likely a bit of sexism at play. People heard it played on the radio and figured, 'Well, women don't talk about masturbation so openly, so it can't be about that. It must be something else that she's touching.' It helps that it's not a raunchy song: it's really a love song. Amphlett is singing about someone with whom she is completely besotted, someone she needs and more than in a sexual way, as evidenced by lines such as 'I forget myself/I want you to remind me'.

Songwriter Steinberg always felt that way about the song, that it was about more than just self-pleasure. 'What I like about the song is that in spite of the fact that the chorus kind of boldly says that, the verse was much more sort of poetic and kind of meaningful,' he said. 'It says, "I love myself, I want you to love me, when I feel down I want you above me, I search myself, I want you to find me, I forget myself, I want you to remind me." Those words, I think, are very strong and it's not an obvious start to finish jack-off song.'

In later years it became much more than just a jack-off song. In 2007 Amphlett was diagnosed with multiple sclerosis. Three years later she felt something wasn't right with her breast although repeated tests were negative for cancer, but Amphlett was convinced something was wrong and opted for a biopsy. That was when cancer was discovered. 'It's shit and it's unfair,' she said, 'but life is not fair – even rock stars get breast cancer. [T]here's been many girls before me [who] have dealt with it successfully. It's easy to feel sorry for me but I feel sorry for people who are suffering it alone.'

She wasn't alone: she had husband Charlie Drayton, an American drummer who first met her when he joined the Divinyls. 'What hooked me?' he asked. 'Just that she was Chrissy, you know? I'd never seen sexy in that way and someone who was so full of life and who seemed to be able to talk about anything, and share certain insights and experiences I'd never had a conversation about, and her love of music

I TOUCH MYSELF

— I think music made us and connected us, making us inseparable.'

The multiple sclerosis made undertaking chemotherapy out of the question, and Amphlett passed away on 21 April 2013. One of her dying wishes was that her song 'I Touch Myself' would be used to raise awareness of the early detection of breast cancer. 'Chrissy wanted to live, and it was breast cancer that broke her body down,' Drayton said. '"I Touch Myself" spoke louder every day from that moment that we confirmed her intuition had been right. Chrissy may not have thought at the time that the song was ever going to relate to breast cancer, but she wants people to live and that means women and men giving themselves the chance to be more aware.'

A year after her death, the I Touch Myself Project was launched with a video featuring Australian singers including Olivia Newton-John, Patricia Amphlett, Deborah Conway, Connie Mitchell, Sarah Blasko and Suze DeMarchi singing 'I Touch Myself'. The stark black and white video, which features each singer staring directly into the camera and singing a few lines, turns the song into a more sombre affair than the Amphlett original – which is totally understandable. 'Now, of course, it's taken on a totally different meaning,' Newton-John said. 'I love the whole reasoning behind doing this song. I'm really sad that she isn't here to sing it with us, and being a breast cancer thriver myself it has an extra meaning for me to do this for her.' Newton-John had been battling breast cancer since a 1992 diagnosis. It came back twice, in 2013 and 2017; she was dealing with it when she sang 'I Touch Myself' for the breast cancer awareness video. The singer lost her own fight on 8 August 2022. 💥

CHAPTER 7

Down Under

MEN AT WORK

In a way *Spicks and Specks* was to blame. In 2007 the popular ABC music quiz show aired a children's music edition. Team leader Alan Brough got to pick one of four categories to be quizzed on, and he picked Nursery Rhymes. One of the questions asked by host Adam Hills was 'Name the Australian nursery rhyme this riff has been based on as well as the name of the man playing it.'

A snatch of 'Down Under' was played, with the focus on the flute part. Red Wiggle Murray Cook identified the song correctly and Greg Ham as the flautist, but no one on the panel could guess the nursery rhyme. Hills offered some help by highlighting the specific section. New Zealand actor and *Play School* host Jay Laga'aia eventually got it, though even he wasn't sure. 'Kookaburra sitting... in the old gum tree?' he said, more as a question than an answer. He was right, and that's when things went wrong for Men at Work.

The next day, then–managing director of Larrikin Music Publishing Norm Lurie arrived at work to find a stack of emails about the show. 'Do you know about this?' they all asked. As owner of the copyright of that song it was a valid question, though it's also odd that no one at the company had noticed the similarity between 'Kookaburra' and the 'Down Under' riff before then. A lawsuit was soon launched alleging copyright infringement – a lawsuit former bandmates felt contributed to Ham's decision to take his own life in 2015.

When the band started there were only two men at work, and they weren't called 'Men at Work': they were called Col and Ron, the first names of Hay and Strykert. They'd met when both were working in Sydney on the stage musical *Heroes*. Over time the duo grew into a band, bringing on board drummer Jerry Speiser, bassist John Rees and musical all-rounder Ham.

Under the name Men at Work they released their first single, 'Keypunch Operator'. The band itself had to put it out because it couldn't get record-company interest. While the band's sound later had tinges of reggae, 'Keypunch Operator' lays that genre on quite heavily. Flip the seven-

inch single over and you'll find a little tune called 'Down Under', but it's not the same version everyone is familiar with. This one is slower and more bass driven than the song that stormed the charts a few years later, but the flute riff that would one day cause problems is still there.

The song came out of one of the first writing sessions Hay and Strykert had. Strykert got the idea to fill some empty beer bottles with water to various levels and see what tunes he could play. He recorded the results, and while Hay was playing the tape in his car the chorus of 'Down Under' came to him. 'It's a very important song for me,' Hay said. 'It always felt like a strong song right from the start. Originally the idea came from a little bass riff that Ron had recorded on a little home cassette demo. It was just a little bass riff with some percussion that he played on bottles [that] were filled with water.

'It was a very intriguing little groove. I really loved it; it had a real trance-like quality to it. I used to listen to it in the car all the time. When I was driving along one day in Melbourne the chorus popped out and a couple of days later I wrote the verses.'

After some solid gigging in their Melbourne base, largely at the Cricketers Arms Hotel in Richmond, the band built enough of a following and enough songs to pique the interest of CBS Records. Signing with a multinational label fit right in with the band's ambitions to become an international act, and it was for that reason the band didn't have any interest in Australian label Mushroom. 'When CBS came along,' Hay said, 'they were the only label interested in us – and that suited us. They were a multinational. We weren't really interested in having a deal with Mushroom. We'd seen that they hadn't had any success internationally.'

Men at Work signed with CBS in early 1981, and by the middle of the year they watched as their major-label debut single 'Who Can It Be Now?' went to No. 1 in Australia. The follow-up was a reworked version of 'Down Under', which followed in the footsteps of the first single. A week later the album *Business As Usual* came out, and that too went to No. 1 on the Australian charts.

Much like Americans have misunderstood the meaning of Bruce Springsteen's 'Born in the USA', believing it to be a patriotic song, what Hay was getting at in the lyrics for 'Down Under' has been missed by Australians – which is somewhat understandable. On the surface it seems to be a song about an Australian travelling abroad and bumping into other Australians; the famous Vegemite sandwich reference really happened to Hay, he once said. There appears to be a sense of pride in coming from the land down under and there is that in the song, but Hay positioned it as more of a lament for the country than praise. To him it was about what Australia was at risk of losing in the 1980s.

'The lyrics are really about my belief about what Australia was becoming,' Hay told the Songfacts website. 'Really, the selling of Australia, in many ways, none of them particularly pleasant, with the overdevelopment of the country. It was what I was feeling at that particular time. It was really a song about the loss of spirit of that country, because it's truly an awesome place. It's difficult to explain and it's very hard for me to put into a sentence. It's been a while since I thought about this, but it's just really about the plundering of the country by greedy people.' The plundering of the country, with added references to chunder and being stoned: the 'head full of zombie' line is a reference to a strong crop of marijuana that was going around Australia at the time.

A song about Australia going to the top of the charts in Australia isn't all that surprising, but it was a surprise to see 'Down Under' go to No. 1 in the United States and even more of a surprise to have *Business As Usual* occupy the same spot in the album

DOWN UNDER 65

charts at the same time. The pair also occupied those positions in the UK at the same time, something The Beatles were one of the only other acts to achieve.

There was a confluence of factors that saw Men at Work become huge in the United States. Some have suggested the band's success was because The Police, a band they were criticised for copying, didn't have an album in the marketplace in 1982, the year *Business As Usual* was released in the US. The idea here was that Men at Work filled in a gap left by The Police, which is a simplistic explanation and one often put forward by Americans who tend to have difficulty picking the difference between an Australian and English accent.

What was an actual factor in Men at Work's success was MTV. The music video channel was growing to cover the nation in 1982 and was hungry for clips to fill its 24-hour broadcast schedule. With Australia and the UK ahead of the game when it came to shooting videos, it meant those bands went into high rotation on the network. While UK pop-star band Duran Duran was all about looking cool in their expensive movie-like clips, Men at Work brought a quirky sense of fun to their videos. It was something quite different from what other bands were offering, and it helped Men at Work stand out in the crowd.

That sense of fun was also present in their TV interviews while touring the US, which further appealed to the local audience, and it helped that Australia was on its way to becoming the flavour of the month in the United States. Not long after Men at

AUSSIE ROCK ANTHEMS

Work's success came Olivia Newton-John's fashionable Koala Blue clothing store, Paul Hogan's shrimp on the barbie commercial and then his *Crocodile Dundee* film.

Then there was Australia's successful 1983 America's Cup campaign, for which 'Down Under' was adopted as a theme song by the crew of *Australia II*. There was also the neat tie-in with the Ben Lexcen–designed winged keel: it was what was down under that counted.

Men at Work made a mistake by rush releasing their follow-up album *Cargo* while *Business As Usual* still had some momentum in the US; the debut was released there more than a year after everywhere else. 'We should have waited,' Hay later admitted. 'It didn't matter when we released that [second] album, people would still have wanted it. We were still selling a shitload of albums. We should have listened [to CBS].'

Despite being a rushed album, *Cargo* performed well. It reached No. 1 in Australia and No. 3 in the US and the single 'Overkill' went to No. 3 on the American charts, but the rot had set in for Men at Work. The fame and attention led to increased infighting in the band, especially between Hay and Speiser. 'Men's communication skills are pretty unsophisticated in their 20s,' Hay later said. 'To have a psychologist on the road would have been great, someone to sort through these things.'

By the time the US tour came to an end Hay had realised he wasn't enjoying working with the other members and wanted to go solo, but the band's manager talked him out of leaving. Instead, they sacked Speiser and Rees ahead of recording the band's third album, *Two Hearts*. Strykert decided to leave during the recording sessions, leaving just Hay and Ham to finish the record and promote it. The album didn't reach the same heights Men at Work had climbed over the previous two years, briefly reaching No. 16 in Australia and No. 50 in the United States. By that time Ham had decided it was all too hard and he also left. After being the biggest band in the world for a while in 1983, by 1985 Men at Work was gone.

At least until that lawsuit that has somewhat tarnished the band's legacy finally reared its ugly head in 2009. Larrikin Music took the 'Down Under' songwriters Hay and

Strykert to court, claiming a whopping 40 to 60 per cent of future royalties and a similar amount dating back to 2002. Before the court could decide on the similarities between 'Down Under' and 'Kookaburra' it had to work out whether Larrikin actually owned the copyright in the first place. That was a little murky, with 'Kookaburra' songwriter Marion Sinclair having written the song in 1932 for a Girl Guides competition. The path wasn't clear: did the Girl Guides own the song because it was their competition, or was it still Sinclair's? The court ruled that it had passed into Girl Guides hands, who had bequeathed it to the State Library of South Australia – and that's where Larrikin picked it up for the sum of $6100.

In terms of whether the 'Kookaburra' riff was filched by Men at Work, on the surface it seemed the answer had to be 'No.' 'Down Under' was a hit in the 1980s and become an iconic Australian song, yet no one had noticed any similarities with 'Kookaburra'. As Hay pointed out, Sinclair herself was alive when 'Down Under' climbed to No. 1 and she didn't pick up on any apparent similarities. Then, of course, there was that episode of *Spicks and Specks* in which none of the six panellists could spot the 'Kookaburra' reference even though the category of Nursery Rhymes really narrowed down their options.

In terms of copyright, that's not the main issue. What matters is objective similarity: when the parts of those two songs are compared, do they sound the same? In his Federal Court ruling Justice Peter Jacobson decided they did but Larrikin didn't get the big payday they were hoping for. 'I consider the figures put forward by Larrikin to be

excessive, over-reaching and unrealistic,' Justice Jacobson ruled, instead ordering 5 per cent of royalties be paid.

The band attempted to appeal the ruling but was rejected, though the appeals judge expressed some disquiet about the concepts of modern copyright that had led to the original decision. In the end, nobody really won. Obviously the band lost, having to pay out royalties to Larrikin, but Larrikin gave themselves a black eye in the process because vocal public opinion was against them. Former Larrikin owner Warren Fahey was caught in the crossfire as people berated him under the mistaken impression that he still owned the business. Fahey had in fact warned Larrikin boss Lurie against going to court. 'I thought that would be a very poor show and produce a very poor outcome,' Fahey said.

The most tragic outcome was the death of flautist Ham two years after the court ruling. While his slide into poor health and depression had started before the court case, it certainly made an already bad situation worse. 'I'm terribly disappointed that that's the way I'm going to be remembered – for copying something,' he said. 'It will be the way the song is remembered and I hate that.'

As for *Spicks and Specks*'s role in inadvertently starting the whole thing, Adam Hills told culture website NME that he still can't listen to the song without feeling remorse. 'What was worst about it was Colin Hay and I were friends,' Hills said. 'We've kind of spoken about it, and I wouldn't say it's ended the friendship, but it's made things ridiculously awkward between us. It's such a weird thing to have happened – that a throwaway question on a music quiz show leads to a court case. I don't think anyone saw that happening. It's such an iconic, beloved Australian song, but I'll never hear it without knowing that I've got this awful connection to it.'

Chances are you've never heard this song, or at least not the original version. The one most people have heard is the remixed version by Filthy Lucre, which included two members of 1980s band I'm Talking. That remix omits some of the most powerful lyrics in the song such as:

This land was never given up
This land was never bought and sold
The planting of the Union Jack
Never changed our law at all.

The remix came about when Melbourne DJ Gavin Campbell was poached by Yothu Yindi's label Mushroom to create some dance remixes. They directed him to Yothu Yindi's two albums, and 'Treaty' stood out to him. 'It sounds like a perfect protest song from an Indigenous Australian act, I reckon, the funkiness and rawness of it,' Campbell said.

Released in 1991, the song was inspired by a 1988 event when Prime Minister Bob Hawke visited the Barunga Festival in the Northern Territory. There he was handed the Barunga Statement, which called for self-management by First Nations people, land rights, compensation for the loss of land and an end to discrimination. 'We call on the Australian Government to support Aborigines in the development of an international declaration of principles for indigenous rights, leading to an international covenant,' the Barunga Statement concluded. 'And we call on the Commonwealth Parliament to negotiate with us a treaty recognising our prior ownership, continued occupation and sovereignty and affirming our human rights and freedom.'

After receiving the Barunga Statement, Hawke raised the idea of a treaty with First Nations people – and his words really left no wiggle room. 'There shall be a treaty negotiated between the Aboriginal people and the government on behalf of all the people of Australia. And secondly, that the next step is that you, the Aboriginal people, should decide what it is that you want to see in that treaty. It's been too long, far too long in achieving, or even being able to think that we will reach that position.'

It was a promise that came after several years of problems with framing a national policy on land rights. However, those years brought the Aboriginal and Torres Strait Islander Commission and the Royal Commission into Aboriginal Deaths in Custody. The treaty promised by Hawke never came to pass, though a 68-page draft treaty was believed to have been created that has not yet been publicly released. This was what prompted Mandawuy Yunupingu to write a song that would become iconic.

Yunupingu started his Western music journey in a David Bowie–inspired covers band in Yirrkala, a small community in the East Arnhem Region of the Northern Territory. Tagged Diamond Dogs, the late 1970s band featured Yunupingu and his two brothers running through songs from the likes of Creedence Clearwater Revival, The Beatles, Elvis Presley and The Rolling Stones. Yunupingu studied education at university and later hooked up with Yirrkala local Witiyana Marika. In part it was likely because Yunupingu liked the way he looked, Matt Garrick wrote in the band's biography. 'Plenty of pimped-up rock and rollers spend years carefully cultivating their image,' Garrick wrote. 'But, for Witiyana . . . rockstar swagger flows as naturally out of his being as fish swim along East Arnhem's Cato River.'

The pair combined Yunupingu's vocals and guitar with Marika on traditional vocals, didgeridoo, clapsticks and dance to make the nucleus of a band. In 1986, a stranger blew into town and really captured their attention. Midnight Oil was touring through the outback on a trip that would permanently change the band and inspire their *Diesel And Dust* album, but it wasn't the tall, bald, gangly frontman of the Oils who caught the attention of the local pair. They were more interested in the support act Warumpi Band, in particular their livewire singer George Rrurrambu Burarrwanga: his Mick Jagger–like swagger made him an ideal frontman.

The bands set up on a truck trailer on the lawns of the Yirrkala church, and Yunupingu and Marika were there to see the show. That swagger of Rrurrambu caught the eye of Yunupingu and Witiyana, but it wasn't just that: it was how he was taking contemporary rock and combining it with the tradition of his people. 'So he's the one who we were inspired by,' Witiyana said.

72 AUSSIE ROCK ANTHEMS

Around that time the pair took to the stage to jam with balanda (white person, or European) Northern Territory act The Swamp Jockeys during the sound check. 'We just went "Wow, you guys are hot!"' Swamp Jockey bassist Stu Kellaway said. 'Like, "They're great songs, just come back later on."'

Swamp Jockeys had pushed forward the Northern Territory music scene, preferring to play originals in places where every pub had a blues band and 'just the same old shit', Kellaway said. He said the Swamp Jockeys were one of the first bands in Darwin to write and play originals in a music scene heavy with covers but, rather than an action solely driven by artistic motivations, Kellaway admitted the band wasn't too crash hot when it came to learning other people's songs.

The balanda members were also very supportive of land rights. 'It was very close to us in the Northern Territory,' one of the band's two singers, Todd Williams, said. 'It was news all the time. We brushed up against some really hardcore bigots and racists [who] we went to school with, but at the same time we grew up with Aboriginal people as well.'

In the mid-1980s Yunupingu was studying in Darwin and went out to see bands, which put him in the orbit of The Swamp Jockeys. They soon became friends, and he took the stage for a few songs when The Swamp Jockeys's pair of singers took a breather. He invited Marika up to Darwin for a few gigs, which soon saw them included as special guests on band posters. They even joined the band on a tour of Sydney pubs.

Swamp Jockeys' drummer Andrew Belletty was awestruck when he watched the band

TREATY 73

performing in Sydney beer barns in front of notoriously tough crowds that wouldn't back away from telling a band just how crap it was. Instead, they impressed, singing in traditional song and language and perhaps leaving a few dropped jaws in their wake. No one would have come to the big smoke and sung like that before.

While playing in the band was fun and the band had been gigging relentlessly, there wasn't a lot of money being made by The Swamp Jockeys. An attempt to record and release an album was tied up in contractual issues and wasn't released. In time, singers Williams and Michael Wyatt decided they'd had enough. Wyatt decided that after spending four years trying to make it in the music industry and not getting as far as he might have liked, he didn't have the dedication to go for four more.

He'd also met a woman who would become his wife, so he decided he couldn't do it anymore. He left, and Williams followed soon after. A band losing its singer can be

the beginning of the end, but in this case there were two ready-made replacements: Yunupingu and Marika. 'They decided we should make one band,' Marika said. 'They knew that we should give a chance for a Yolngu balanda band, a mix, and that's called Yothu Yindi. Doesn't matter, black or white, you still Yothu Yindi. The meaning kinda changed.'

The name 'Yothu Yindi' literally translates to 'mother and child'. It was used as a kinship term referring to the connection the Yolngu clans of north-east Arnhem Land have between themselves. When the pair signed up with the remnants of The Swamp Jockeys, the balanda members were included in that kinship.

The new band released their first album, *Homeland Movement*, in 1989 and it charted at No. 59. Working on songs for their follow-up, Yunupingu had a chat around a campfire with a guy named Paul Kelly. Yes, *that* Paul Kelly. Their paths had first crossed when both were on separate tours in the US. On a night off, Kelly went to see a Midnight Oil gig where Yothu Yindi was the support act. He went backstage, the two got to chatting and a friendship developed.

That campfire in Arnhem Land some time in 1990 was 12 months after Hawke's promise of a treaty, and Yunupingu said all the talk seemed to have died down. 'I said, "I want to write a song that is centred on treaty",' Yunupingu told triple j's Richard Kingsmill. 'So we started playing around with some lyrics. My lyrics at the time were that I'd heard it on the radio and I saw it on the television, but where is it? Where's the treaty?'

Kelly remembered the song coming slowly; his normal approach to songwriting wasn't to go from the top down. For some songwriters the inspiration can't be corralled but has to lead the way. The pair eventually got parts of the song together and decided to head to Darwin to work on it with the rest of the band. That move turned out to be the right one, because it spawned one of the iconic moments of the song.

'We were jamming on the last day, the band was jamming on a groove,' Kelly said. 'We only had one verse that we'd written for "Treaty" and they started singing those lines over the top. For want of nothing better to do, we sang "Treaty, yeah, treaty, now" over

the top of the groove. We thought, "Maybe there's something there" and recorded it on a little beatbox in the middle of the room.'

There was something there, a chant that ended up featuring in the Filthy Lucre remix that drove the song up the charts. However, the song still wasn't finished. Sometime later the band travelled to Melbourne to record the album, and Kelly got a call from the manager saying they'd recorded 'Treaty'. This was a surprise to Kelly, because he didn't think the song was complete.

The manager said there was interest in releasing the song as a single, though there was a problem: no one could understand the words. Kelly knew that was because the song hadn't been finished yet; Yunupingu was just mumbling a melody. He and Yunupingu later met up to finish the song in Sydney, visiting a nearby friend to get his opinion. 'We walked around the corner to the Midnight Oil office and played what we had to Peter [Garrett],' Kelly said. 'He suggested some arrangement things, some good ideas. They recorded it the next day with Peter in the studio.'

Garrett wasn't the only guest in the studio: also providing backing vocals for the song were Archie Roach, Split Enz's Tim Finn and Rose Bygrave from Goanna. Finn's vocal track is quite prominent in the

AUSSIE ROCK ANTHEMS

remix; it's his voice singing 'Treaty, yeah, treaty, now'. Once you know that it's easy to recognise his voice.

It was a significant moment when the original version of 'Treaty' was released as a single in 1991: it was perhaps the first time a charting single featured a First Nations language so prominently. 'We hadn't heard this call coming from Aboriginal voices, particularly with language,' Garrett said, 'and we never had experienced that call broadcast to such a wide audience once "Treaty" became played lot on radio.'

What really got the song going was the Filthy Lucre remix, which stripped away most of the verses, kept the memorable chorus and added a thumping beat. 'That was the song that went up the charts and was played in clubs all over the world,' Kelly said. 'I remember everywhere you went in those days the song was playing and people would jump on the dancefloor as soon as it came on.'

The original version of 'Treaty' didn't chart, but the remix proved so popular it went to No. 11 in Australia and also charted in Belgium, The Netherlands, the United Kingdom and the US. Producer Mark Moffatt remembered a particular moment when he realised just how much difference the song was making. He was sitting in Melbourne's Tullamarine airport just after 'Treaty' had hit the record stores, back when such things still existed. A bunch of white kids came up and asked the band for their autographs. Moffat thought, *Hang on, something is really happening here*.

In part because of his work in Yothu Yindi and as a school principal and educator in Yirrkala, Yunupingu was named the 1992 Australian of the Year. It came 11 months after he had been refused entry to a St Kilda bar for being inappropriately dressed: he was wearing jeans, Doc Martens and a long-sleeved collared shirt bought for around $60. 'The bloke who was trying to get us out of the joint kept saying that,' Yunupingu said, 'but I felt that it was only because there was a racist attitude. I could feel that, I could see that.' The bar manager later denied any discrimination.

While that sent one message that perhaps reconciliation might be some way off, just a month before Yunupingu accepted the Australian of the Year award Prime

Minister Paul Keating made his powerful Redfern Address. It was the first time an Australian prime minister had faced head-on the realities and damage of colonialism.

'Isn't it reasonable to say that if we can build a prosperous and remarkably harmonious multicultural society in Australia, surely we can find just solutions to the problems [that] beset the first Australians – the people to whom the most injustice has been done,' Keating said. 'The starting point might be to recognise that the problem starts with

AUSSIE ROCK ANTHEMS

us non-Aboriginal Australians. It begins, I think, with that act of recognition. Recognition that it was we who did the dispossessing. We took the traditional lands and smashed the traditional way of life. We brought the diseases. The alcohol. We committed the murders. We took the children from their mothers. We practised discrimination and exclusion. It was our ignorance and our prejudice. And our failure to imagine these things being done to us.' They were strong words about what had occurred in our past that to this day some still don't have any interest in facing.

When Keating presented Yunupingu with his award the musician showed his ability to see past what had gone on before – not to forget it happened, but in recognition that it was the key to moving forward. 'I feel as if I'm Yolngu first, it comes from my heart. "Australian" is just a label put on to what has happened in the past, but I'll always be Yolngu,' he said. 'Australia is just 200 years old. What I believe is we were a nation before another nation took over: that's what adds strength to what I believe in. I'm proud to be an Australian, because this is the best country in the world. The colonisation that happened, with the laws and religion and oppression and our people becoming victims of that oppression, are part of history. But I tend to look beyond that – to stopping being a victim. Things will change.'

As radio shock jock Alan Jones showed just a few days later, change might be slow in coming. Jones demonstrated he hadn't got the memo or even noted it was the International Year for the World's Indigenous People. Clearly not being able to comprehend what Yunupingu had done, Jones declared he got the award because he was a First Nations man. 'To promote people because of their colour or their history rather than their merit is the most intolerable form of racism, which givers of such an award say they oppose,' Jones said, though those subject to racism would surely be able to supply more 'intolerable' examples. Not surprisingly, it cast a pall over Yunupingu. According to Garrick's biography, a teacher at his school remembered him 'walking around in the same depressed state as he was after being branded a "coon" at a Northern Territory principals' conference years earlier'.

He recorded and released four more albums with Yothu Yindi and continued his work as a teacher. In 2007 he announced he was suffering advanced kidney failure brought on, in part, by diabetes and high blood pressure. A year later he had resigned himself to the likelihood that he may not live to see that treaty he'd sung about. 'I'm still waiting for that treaty to come along, for my grandsons,' he told *The Australian*. 'Even if it's not there in the days that I am living, it might come in the days that I am not living. I know a treaty will change things, my grandsons will have a different view, a much more positive view, a luckier view. Luckier in that they feel part of Australia, you know.'

Mandawuy Yunupingu passed away on 2 June 2013.

Those words above, which still hold out hope that a treaty will one day come, featured on a plaque unveiled in his honour in 2018 at Birany Birany in East Arnhem.

CHAPTER 9

How To Make Gravy

PAUL KELLY

In a way we have James Blundell to thank for this song. Starting in 1993, every year Myer put out a *Spirit of Christmas* CD to raise money for the Salvation Army (the last edition was in 2018). Organised by Lindsay Fields, a member of John Farnham's band, it saw popular artists recording a Christmas tune. The likes of Farnham, Olivia Newton-John, Jimmy Barnes, James Reyne and Marina Prior had contributed songs over the years.

Paul Kelly was approached to take part in the 1996 release, the fourth in the series, for which the proceeds would go to the Starlight Foundation. His first choice was a cover of The Band's 'Christmas Must Be Tonight', but Blundell had recorded that two years earlier. Kelly told Fields he'd have a crack at writing his own Christmas song; after all, he went all right at this songwriting caper. He'd had the bones of a tune the band had been kicking around at soundcheck for a while, but no words had appeared to join it. An avowed fan of Christmas songs, Kelly gave the record *A Christmas Gift For You From Phil Spector* a spin on the morning of 25 December every year. The first song on that album is a version of Irving Berlin's 'White Christmas' sung by Darlene Love.

While everyone knows the song, it includes a spoken section that is often left out of other versions. In it, the singer tells us that while it's a gloriously sunny day in LA, it's Christmas Eve, so they are longing for the cold north.

Even a search for the lyrics on Google will throw up plenty of instances where this verse is left out. Love put this verse in the middle of the song but Berlin originally had it at the start, which was inspired by a Broadway tradition. 'Berlin was hewing to the Tin Pan Alley convention of preceding 32-bar choruses with six measures of mood-setting introduction,' Jody Rosen wrote in her book on the song. 'On the Broadway stage, these verses served a similar function to the recitative that precedes an operatic aria; they were often performed conversationally – a casual way of establishing the tempo and dynamics of a song and easing into its refrain.' Berlin seemed conflicted about this verse: when it was released in 1942 he

where Kelly drew his inspiration. Maybe the focus of his Christmas song should be about *not* being where you want to be. 'I was thinking that if you're away from something you imagine it more intensely,' he said.

The idea of protagonist Joe being in jail rather than, say, being at work or overseas didn't seem to be a conscious decision. 'It was a way to write the song,' Kelly said. 'One minute I was thinking "This guy's got to be away." Next thing I knew he was in prison. I was trying to write about Christmas. I wasn't trying to write about being in prison, but I guess it ended up being a bit of both.'

Kelly later looked back at the song and wondered if this was the first time Joe turned up in one of his songs. '"To Her Door", then "Love Never Runs On Time" and "How To Make Gravy": I've got a feeling it's the same guy. He keeps coming back. He's a bit of a fuck-up, that guy.'

When he finished writing the song Kelly called Fields and said: 'I have a Christmas song, but it doesn't have a chorus and it's set in prison.' Fields figured he'd better go over to Kelly's place and have a listen. The

ordered it expunged from the sheet music, but in 1989 he wrote to singer Rosemary Clooney to thank her for including it in a live performance.

When that introduction is taken into account it changes the nature of the song. Without it 'White Christmas' seems happy, the thoughts of someone fondly remembering past festive seasons. With it the song becomes one with a tinge of sadness, the narrator singing about all the things they're missing – and that's next day Fields sat in Kelly's back shed with the songwriter looking down at his notebook containing the freshly scratched lyrics. Looking down meant Kelly didn't have to deal with the nerves of seeing Fields's reaction until he'd finished the song.

When he looked up Fields had tears in his eyes, which confused Kelly a bit. 'It's supposed to be a comedy,' he said to Fields. Kelly can have a different view on his own tunes sometimes: 'When I First Met Your Ma' is a song about him describing to his son the courtship of his mother and eventual separation. When the band first heard it they thought it was the saddest song ever, but Kelly told them he thought it was funny.

Fields liked 'How To Make Gravy' but still had to get the song over the line with the Myer board, given it was quite a bit different from usual fare such as 'Little Drummer Boy'. The board gave it the tick and it ended up as track five on the CD, alongside Farnham, Reyne, Judith Durham and the one-minute wonder that was CDB.

That Christmas Kelly also released it as a four-track EP, and it appeared on his greatest hits collection *Songs From The South*, released mid-1997. It was nominated for Song of the Year at the 1997 ARIAs, losing to Savage Garden's 'To The Moon And Back'. In 1998 it was nominated in the same category at the Australasian Performing Right Association awards, where it again lost – this time to Leonardo's Bride's 'Even When I'm Sleeping'.

Born in Adelaide, Kelly's music career didn't really begin until a move to Melbourne. There he found himself fronting an act called The High Rise Bombers, developing

HOW TO MAKE GRAVY   85

both his songwriting chops and his skills as a frontman. In time his ambition came to the fore: he tried to change the band's name to Paul Kelly and the High Rise Bombers, complete with a poster in which he stood on his own in the centre with the rest of the band shunted to tiny headshots across the top, and insisting they would only play his songs. The second stipulation was a bold move given another High Rise Bomber was Martin Armiger, who became the songwriter for The Sports and spent decades as a composer for film and TV.

After The High Rise Bombers, Kelly joined The Dots. History repeated itself there: they became Paul Kelly and the Dots and the focus was on his material. The Dots released two albums, both of which are collector's items due to the fact that in later years Mushroom Records owner Michael Gudinski gave Kelly the rights to some of his back catalogue. Kelly decided to not make those albums available because he found them embarrassing to listen to. It's hard not to feel sorry for the other Dots members, knowing that people can no longer hear the albums they played on.

In 1984 The Dots were done and Kelly moved from St Kilda to Kings Cross (yes, by bus; the song of that name is true). In Sydney he recorded what became *Post*, his first solo album. With Mushroom not excited about it he started shopping it around, but then trusted Gudinski employee Michelle Higgins stepped in. She wanted Kelly to stay on the label and told Gudinski she had checked into a fancy hotel on Mushroom's dime and would stay there until Kelly was re-signed. Gudinski buckled and Kelly stayed.

For the *Post* follow-up Kelly wanted to record a double album, an audacious move given the first album didn't sell or get much radio play. Gudinski initially baulked, but later reluctantly consented. That double album was 1986's *Gossip*, the record that saw Kelly and his band the Coloured Girls break through courtesy of songs such as 'Before Too Long' and 'Darling It Hurts'. The Coloured Girls band released three more studio albums, the last after they changed their name to The Messengers as they were known in the US due to racial undertones, before Kelly decided their time was up. From then on Kelly recorded solo albums while also working on side projects with Professor Ratbaggy, The Stormwater Boys, Stardust Five and Charlie Owen.

Before the first of the side projects came along Kelly recorded 'How To Make Gravy' in 1996. Despite the ARIA and APRA nominations the song itself wasn't an instant smash: it was a slow burner, though by 2010 it was well known enough for Kelly to use it as the title of his 'mongrel memoir'. In 2017 he launched what has become a December tradition, the 'How To Make Gravy' tour, where he brings along younger acts such as Meg Mac, Amyl and the Sniffers, Gang of Youths and Alex the Astronaut. It has also spawned its own day: 21 December is Gravy Day, when social media goes crazy with the #gravyday hashtag.

HOW TO MAKE GRAVY 87

With the COVID-19 pandemic the song made stronger connections with people as lockdowns and the like meant they couldn't be with their family for Christmas. In 2021, after a year or more of lockdown, Kelly released a new version of the song as part of his *Christmas Train* double album. 'The original "How To Make Gravy" came out 25 years ago and I must have played it now thousands and thousands of times,' Kelly said of this version. 'It's a staple in our set. The band and I thought it would be worthwhile putting our current version to tape. The way we play the song has evolved over the years, but not that much.

'We've always kept the crucial slide riff, originally played by Spencer P. Jones, and on this recording by Ashley Naylor. Playing this song is like going on a ride. Once you're on it, it just takes off!'

Accompanying it was a video made by his partner Siân Darling that still tugs at the heartstrings. Made up of a string of self-filmed clips of people holding up messages to tell loved ones they miss them or singing along to the song, there are quite a few tears both from those in the video and those watching.

Part of the lasting appeal of the song is that there are very few Australian Christmas tunes that aren't a bit naff. What 'How To Make Gravy' does is focus on the celebration around the day: the siblings driving or flying to the family home, the brothers- and sisters-in-law turning up along

AUSSIE ROCK ANTHEMS

with other relatives, the food and the post-lunch dancing (though after a big meal most people would rather doze than dance). It's an image that is familiar to most Australians as it reflects the reality of what most of us do every Christmas. 'Christmas was a big part of my childhood,' Kelly said. 'I had a big Catholic family, so Christmas has always been about family getting together and we sang carols over the years. That was part of the tradition for us to get together on Christmas Eve and sing carols and Christmas songs like "Jingle Bell Rock" [and] "Rudolph the Red Nosed Reindeer".'

With most of those Christmas tunes you listen to them in December but then shelve them for the rest of the year. As Christmas songs go, 'How To Make Gravy' is very understated: in five minutes and 10 seconds it only mentions the word 'Christmas' three times. It's not an overt Christmas song so it doesn't feel odd to listen to it at other times of the year. Who listens to 'Jingle Bell Rock' in March?

One mystery of the song is just how Joe is communicating with Dan. It's often thought to be a phone call, and there are instances that suggest that. The signs of that include the opener 'Hey, Dan, it's Joe', which is very much the way a phone call begins. There's also the moment when he mentions his concerns about Dan making a move on Rita, phrasing that certainly seems like words coming out of Joe's mouth before he realises and has to quickly blurt out an apology.

The reference to ringing the last bells in the second line calls the possibility of a phone call into question. Presumably the last bells are a sign the cells are about to be locked, and it's hard to imagine Joe being able to make a phone call that late. Also, Joe goes for five minutes from that point and it's unlikely the prison guards would be standing near the phones patiently waiting for him to finish.

Overall, the feel of the song is more suggestive of a letter being written, especially because the conversation is entirely one way. Dan's voice never appears, not even to comfort his brother that they'll work out the gravy situation. The problem with the letter hypothesis is that he's writing it on the night of 21 December. The earliest it could be posted is 22 December, assuming Joe finished the letter the night before. That only allows two days for the letter to get from prison to Dan's house so he can get the message to kiss Joe's kids on Christmas Day. That short turnaround seems rather unlikely.

Perhaps that's the point: 'How To Make Gravy' is about not being somewhere, about missing out. Joe's letter finally arriving days after Christmas fits in with that theme of him missing out, and his family would have missed out on the gravy he felt was so important.

Incidentally, the recipe mentioned in the song? That's real: it comes from Kelly's first father-in-law.

CHAPTER 10

You're The Voice

★ ★ ★ ★ ★ ★ ★ ★ ★ ★

JOHN FARNHAM

John Farnham luckily avoided recording what became one of the worst songs in rock history while working on his mega-selling comeback album *Whispering Jack*. Not a noted songwriter himself, Farnham needed outside help to find tunes for the album and that job fell largely to his manager Glenn Wheatley, who had to work hard to get people to hand over their tunes. Farnham wasn't a big name in the mid-1980s so there were a lot of famous singers in line ahead of him, and songwriters want their tunes to go to famous singers because there's more of a chance of earning big royalties.

Still, Wheatley did what he could, and it seems he did quite a lot. He ended up bringing back boxes and boxes of demos: at least 3000 songs in all. 'I listened to every one of them right the way through,' Farnham said. 'After a few you do get a bit brain dead, but you can't afford to miss any.'

One of the songs hidden away in those boxes was the justifiably maligned 'We Built This City' with its odd lines such as 'Marconi plays the mamba'. Luckily for Farnham, he passed on that tune. He was lucky because US band Starship was on the verge of releasing it as a single, and while it went to No. 1 in Australia, the United States and several other countries the song went on to acquire a certain infamy. Oddly enough it was co-written by Elton John's lyricist Bernie Taupin, though he insists his version was much darker and blamed an Austrian record producer for changing the song.

'I still don't like that song,' Farnham later explained. 'I just couldn't hear myself singing it; it just didn't appeal to me.' This was fortunate for him: in 2011 a *Rolling Stone* readers' poll voted it the worst song of the 1980s. 'This could be the biggest blow-out victory in the history of the *Rolling Stone* readers poll,' the magazine reported. 'You really, *really* hate "We Built This City" by Starship. It crushed the competition.'

The song also finished in the top spot on *Blender* magazine's 50 most awesomely bad songs ever. 'Over the years, as '80s music began to sound dated and ludicrous – and no song sounds more '80s than "We Built This City" – it developed a hideous

It was worth putting the effort into finding just the right songs, because there was a lot riding on the album that became *Whispering Jack*. Farnham's career was in a lull – he was viewed by many as a has-been from the 1970s – and he was flat broke. After recording the album he didn't even have enough money in his pocket to take his son to McDonald's for his birthday.

It had been quite a fall from the heady days of his early career. Born in England, his family came to Australia via the assisted migrant scheme, which made him a 10-pound Pom. The family settled in Victoria, Farnham finished school and began a plumbing apprenticeship but he was also singing in bands, which is how his first manager Darryl Sambell found him. Farnham signed with Sambell, who marketed him as Johnny Farnham. The first big move was getting him to record 'Sadie, The Cleaning Lady'. Both of them recognised it as a cheesy novelty tune, but it landed him a No. 1 single straight out of the gates. Later it was an albatross around his neck as he tried to revive his career.

Through the 1970s Johnny Farnham released a number of top-10 hits, was named

reputation: the worst song of all time,' *GQ* wrote in an oral history of the song.

Quality notwithstanding, it wasn't the only song Farnham passed on that ended up being a hit for someone else. He also said 'No' to 'From A Distance', which Bette Midler later took to No. 2 on the US *Billboard* charts. '"From A Distance" had quite a pleasant melody,' Farnham explained, 'but I'm not overly religious and the song says "God is watching us". Frankly, I would have felt uncomfortable singing that, because it's not where I'm from.'

AUSSIE ROCK ANTHEMS

King of Moomba in 1972 back when such a thing was a big deal and *TV Week* readers voted him King of Pop five years in a row. He also dabbled in stage musicals, meeting future wife Gillian in one where she was hired as a dancer. As the 1970s came to a close Farnham found he was in a lot of trouble. He was hit with a big bill for unpaid taxes for the previous nine years and a restaurant venture failed. It was a combination of events that sent him broke but also led to him coming under the wing of Wheatley, a manager who showed extraordinary faith in Farnham.

The pair had known each other since the late 1960s, when they became flatmates. Farnham went above and beyond standard flatmate duties for Wheatley's 21st in 1969. Wheatley's mum had sent him a bottle of champagne as a gift, which he absent-mindedly left in his car for too long, and there it sat for hours with the hot sun doing its worst. When Wheatley finally popped the cork and drank the contents he found himself head in the toilet bowl throwing up for quite a few hours. Farnham regularly went in to check on him. 'I saved his life, you know,' Farnham later said. 'I rescued him from drowning in the toilet bowl. We became good mates.'

It could be suggested that Wheatley owed him. Farnham decided to let Wheatley manage him in 1980 and gave notice he was now John Farnham; the boy Johnny Farnham was gone. The attempt to move him away from the teen-star image to one as an adult entertainer started with a cover of The Beatles's 'Help'. Given his dire financial circumstances, it was somewhat autobiographical: Farnham's power ballad version reminded people he had a good set of pipes and they sent it into the top 10.

In 1982 Farnham replaced Glenn Shorrock as lead singer of another Wheatley-managed act, Little River Band. For the cash-strapped singer it must have seemed like a way out into the light. LRB had made it big in the US so surely the money would soon flow, but it wasn't to be the case. By the time Farnham joined, LRB were on a downward trajectory. There were personality clashes that had been well hidden and the band's finances were suffering because of huge recording advances they had received. With album sales not strong enough for the label to recoup those advances, LRB was in debt.

Not even songwriting royalties, which can't be touched by labels, were a gold mine. Farnham penned the catchy 'Playing To Win' but suffered because of the insane way the band calculated royalties. 'The most anal thing that I observed was when they got down to the end of the project,' assistant producer on the 'Playing To Win' sessions, Rand Bishop, said. 'They listened to every song and negotiated writer's shares down to the sub-percentages: like one guy would get 9.14 per cent. They would divide every line of a lyric and every line of music and claim ownership.' In the end Farnham got 55.5 per cent of his own song, easily the best on the album.

YOU'RE THE VOICE

On stage there was friction between Farnham and long-time band members Beeb Birtles and Graeham Goble, who wanted to rein in the new guy. Sometimes that meant giving him just six feet of mic cable to stop him roaming the stage, while at other times his microphone stand was gaffer-taped to the floor. When the label dumped the band in 1986, Farnham took it as his cue to leave. He had found being part of a band where everyone got a say in decisions quite stifling: he wanted to be the one calling the shots. Also, it was impossible to ad-lib during a song when three other members were singing harmonies and expecting the tune to be the same night after night.

Farnham and Wheatley agreed it was time to record a solo album. While Farnham worked on the album Wheatley had the task of signing a record deal, which proved to be a hard ask. Record company after record company passed on Farnham, with that 'Sadie' song in the backs of their minds. Even when Wheatley played the stuff Farnham was working on there were no bites.

Wheatley ended up at the bottom of his list: RCA Records. 'In those days RCA Records was the absolute last resort when it came to record companies,' Wheatley wrote in his autobiography. He played the boss a demo of a song called 'You're The Voice' but still had to throw in his own label, WBE, to sweeten the deal. RCA was keen to acquire a label with local acts such as Real Life and Moving Pictures because they had no Australian acts on their roster.

'Here was a chance for them to change the image and perception of the company in one move,' Wheatley wrote. Farnham signed with RCA, which was a slight relief for Wheatley: he had such faith in what Farnham was doing that he had been paying for the recording sessions. He had even remortgaged his house to pay what was up to that point a $150,000 bill. 'That was a lot for an album in those days,' Wheatley said. 'We had people on the payroll, people employed to look for songs. It was expensive because it took a long time to make. We were getting over John's pop star days.'

While the label had liked what it heard in 'You're The Voice', the last track sourced for the album, Farnham almost hadn't been able to get his hands on the song. Based in

the UK, co-writer Chris Thompson was inspired to write the song after 100,000 people marched to Hyde Park to support the campaign for nuclear disarmament. 'I'd overslept and didn't make the march,' Thompson told Cameron Adams from *The Telegraph*. 'We were watching it on TV. I was annoyed at myself and that's where the idea for "You're the Voice" came from. If you want to do something you have to go out and do it yourself.'

Thompson's label didn't like it, figuring the era of protest songs was over. Farnham felt otherwise: he heard the song and instantly knew it was for him. However, Thompson wasn't too keen on the idea. 'I got a call from my publisher saying "This guy called John Farnham from Australia wants to record 'You're the Voice',"' Thompson told Adams. 'I said, "You've got to be joking! He's not doing it". I'd grown up in New Zealand and all I knew about John Farnham was "Sadie The Cleaning Lady". I told my publisher he's like a joke in Australia and absolutely no way is he recording "You're the Voice" and put the phone down.

YOU'RE THE VOICE 95

'Two hours later I got another call saying, "He really wants to do it, he's making this big comeback record, he wants this for the album." They persuaded me to allow him to record it — my feeling is he'd already recorded it — and if I didn't like it I could say "No."'

It took three days for 'You're the Voice' to be mixed, a lot of time for just one song. It was likely in part due to things such as using the slamming door of a car to replicate the sound of the drums, and maybe the bagpipe solo that had been Farnham's idea. When Wheatley heard it he was disappointed: it didn't give him goosebumps like the demo version had. Farnham read the look on his manager's face and said, 'You don't like it, do you?'

'There's something about the song that isn't as good as the demo,' Wheatley replied.

Farnham said, 'It's the vocal, isn't it?' then rolled up his sleeves and went back to the studio, demanding the lights be turned off and the volume turned up in his headphones. 'He put the headphones on and put in a vocal performance as only John knows how,' Wheatley wrote. 'The experience that night was awesome. Driving home we put the rough mix of his new vocal on in the car and I knew we had a hit.'

Farnham still had his doubts. Keenly aware of how much was riding on the album, he went into a sort of depression after handing over a tape of the finished product to Wheatley with the note 'This is the best I can do. Thanks for the chance. Love, John'. He spent the six weeks until the release holed up in bed at home, rarely surfacing. 'After finishing the album, I didn't feel like eating for two weeks,' he said. 'One time I was literally lying on the lounge room floor in the foetal position, sobbing with fear. It was just awful.' He didn't even want to go to the album's listening party, sobbing in the car and worrying that no one would like it. His wife Gillian told him to get out of the car and go through with it.

Whispering Jack was released in October 1986, with 'You're The Voice' as the first single. Promotion was tricky at first, with some radio stations telling Wheatley 'We don't play *Johnny* Farnham.' However, when one FM station broke ranks the others soon followed, sending the song to No. 1 for six weeks. Despite being released late in the year it became the biggest-selling song of the year, and the album held the top spot for a massive 25 weeks.

Soon afterwards Wheatley was driving in his car with Farnham in the passenger seat. 'You've got to appreciate this,' he said to Farnham. 'As we speak we have the No. 1 album in the country. We have to enjoy this moment.' Farnham didn't say anything, and Wheatley looked over at his mate: tears were streaming down his face. With all the cards stacked against him, Farnham had come through.

In 2023 the song was gifted to the Yes campaign for The Voice referendum as the soundtrack to an ad. It looked at defining moments in Australian history, from the 1967 referendum to including First Nations people in the census, the Mabo decision, the America's Cup and Cathy Freeman's 2000 gold medal. Farnham said: 'This song changed my life. I can only hope that now it might help, in some small way, to change the lives of our First Nations peoples for the better.'

Not everyone welcomed the song's use, with some taking to social media to vent their outrage and post photos of their garbage bins full of Farnham CDs – which they presumably fished out not long after they took the photo.

CHAPTER 11

The Horses

DARYL BRAITHWAITE

Daryl Braithwaite never really wanted to work a day job. He grew up in South Yarra in Victoria and went to school with someone named Olivia Newton-John, before the family moved to Sydney's northern suburbs. He finished school there, and music really started to get its hooks into him. Finishing school in Year 10, his dad pushed him towards a fitter and turner's apprenticeship on Cockatoo Island in Sydney Harbour. That didn't go too well, as he tended to take a day off to go surfing whenever the waves were good. His eternally patient boss realised the kid wasn't interested in the job, so they came to an agreement: Braithwaite got his papers saying he had finished his apprenticeship and the boss got to hire someone who would actually turn up for work.

He was gigging in local bands when he got his big chance in 1970, when Clive Shakespeare from a band called Sherbet asked if he wanted to join. They'd just released their first single, which went nowhere special, but big things were afoot.

Two years later Sherbet had charting hits, appearances on *Countdown* and screaming teenagers everywhere they went. Oh, and there was also a lot of chest hair and satin jackets. However, the good times didn't last forever: the screaming teenagers grew up and their tastes changed, while their younger siblings weren't interested in a hand-me-down pop band because they wanted their own stars to scream at. That and an abortive push into the US market that saw them change their name to Highway signalled the end of Sherbet.

In the 1980s, with a wife and child to support, Braithwaite was on the dole for a while before he found a roadworking gig at the local council. 'I was quite nervous fronting up to Bulla Shire Council and saying "Hi, I'm Daryl Braithwaite, I'm meant to report here and go to work,"' Braithwaite said. 'I can remember the guy looking up at me and going "Right, okay."'

Oddly enough, it gave him the impetus he needed to get back into music again. His fellow roadworkers recognised the guy from all those *Countdown* appearances and asked

him what the hell he was doing there. They *had* to take this job but Braithwaite had a talent, yet there he was spinning a stop-go sign. That led to him working on an album that became *Edge*. Released in late 1988, it didn't race up the charts – in fact, it took six months to get to No. 1 – but it ended up going triple platinum, sold more than 250,000 copies and spawned five singles. Braithwaite was back.

His big moment was still to come, via a song that almost didn't make it onto his follow-up album *Rise*. Near the end of the recording session a friend tipped him off to Rickie Lee Jones's 'Flying Cowboys' long player, an album that opens with a song called 'The Horses'. That's right: it's a cover version, a fact that still seems to surprise some people. 'I remember going home after being in the studio. I got the CD out, put it on and the first track was "The Horses" and I thought "My god, how good is that?" as soon as I heard it.'

Album producer Simon Hussey had to do some work to turn it into a 'Daryl song'. He added an intro and marimba-like sounds and tightened it: Braithwaite's version is around one minute shorter than the original. Hussey also felt it needed a female backing vocalist and called in New Zealander Margaret Urlich. The idea worked so well that Hussey chose to cut out Braithwaite's vocal at some points so Urlich's could shine, turning it into more of a duet.

'The Horses' was the second single released from *Rise* – you never go with a slow song as the first single – and Braithwaite was sent up the New South Wales coast to Sandbar Beach to film a video. One of the things Braithwaite remembered most about the shoot was that he wore a jumper tucked into his pants, which he mentioned in several interviews, but the most unusual thing about the video is that the woman 'singing' isn't Urlich. She was over in London recording and didn't want to fly back for the shoot, so to fill in for her the video maker nabbed model Gillian Bailey and got her to lip-synch Urlich's parts.

Given the ongoing popularity of 'The Horses' it may surprise some to know it wasn't an immediate hit. Released in January 1991, it didn't crack the top 100 until 10 February, when it snuck in at No. 99. Then, rather than disappearing, 'The Horses' kept on hanging around and by April had made its way into the top 10. It slowly made its way along until it got to the No. 1 spot in May, where it stayed for two weeks. It spent 23 weeks in the top 50 and 30 in the top 100, became the fifth-highest-selling song that

100 AUSSIE ROCK ANTHEMS

year and helped take *Rise* to No. 3 on the album charts and go four times platinum, selling 300,000 copies.

That was probably when most people expected 'The Horses' to slowly fade away, becoming the sort of song that might get the occasional spin on a hits and memories FM radio station, but around 2004 something happened. It's hard to say what it was, but that was the year Google showed two huge spikes in people searching for Braithwaite's cover version. Braithwaite himself noticed something special was happening with 'The Horses' at that time. 'We first started to notice it four years ago in Perth,' he told the *Cairns Post* in 2009. 'We did this gig and the first 100 people down the front were all aged between 18 and 25 and we thought "God, what's going on?"' They sang all of the songs off *Edge* and *Rise*, and when we played "The Horses" the whole place erupted.'

The horse-racing community grabbed on to the song, getting Braithwaite to sing it at the W.S. Cox Plate for several years, although there were ructions when some complained that the crowd singalong spooked the horses. In 2013–15 'The Horses' rode on the back of Hawthorn's three-peat as AFL Premiers, and during the first season it became the team victory song.

The resurgence of 'The Horses' was enough to see Sony, which had ditched Braithwaite a decade earlier, re-sign him in 2013. In 2017 he was ushered into the ARIA Hall of Fame for the second time; he was already in there as a member of Sherbet. That same year he also got to sing 'The Horses' with Jones during her Australian tour, when all he wanted to do was say 'Hi.' 'I would have been happy just to have met her,' Braithwaite said. 'I was not expecting to sing with her. She said, "Maybe you take the second verse because I will be playing guitar and I am a bit clunky."' The performance wasn't the best, in part because they were singing Jones's slower and longer version and not Braithwaite's. In the online video footage Braithwaite seems awkward, as though he's trying to predict the tempo of the song and work out where he's supposed to come in.

Watching the video of that performance online, it's conclusive proof that Braithwaite's version of 'The Horses' is much, much better.

THE HORSES

There was very much an international flavour to 'Friday On My Mind', and to The Easybeats as well. While always thought of as an Australian band, all five of the founding members were actually born in Europe and only found themselves in Australia when their families emigrated in the late 1950s and 1960s. Singer Stevie Wright and drummer Gordon 'Snowy' Fleet were from England, rhythm guitarist George Young hailed from Scotland while bassist Dingeman Adriaan Henry van der Sluijs and lead guitarist Johannes Hendrikus Jacob van den Berg were Dutch born. The last two became better known under their anglicised stage names of Dick Diamonde and Harry Vanda.

Several members of the band met at the Villawood Migrant Hostel, with the remainder being found in the nearby suburbs. Ted Albert from Albert Productions soon showed an interest in the band, calling them into the 2UW Theatre in Sydney and telling them to run through all their material. Once he heard an original, 'Say That You're Mine', Albert was hooked; he knew he had to sign them.

Success wasn't immediate: The Easybeats had to wait until they released their second single for everything to go crazy. 'She's So Fine' shot to No. 3, made them famous across the country and spawned a local version of Beatlemania known as Easyfever. It got so crazy that when a music magazine published the Youngs's home address hundreds of fans milled on the street outside. Some even broke into the house.

In 1967 they headed overseas with the view of taking England by storm. 'We had figured on staying there three or four months,' Young told *Rolling Stone*, 'doing a bit of recording, hopefully getting a single out, hopefully getting it on the charts, and make ourselves a lot of dough working through Europe and America.'

It didn't quite work out that way. The first UK single 'Come And See Her' didn't do a whole lot, so the UK label hooked them up with visiting US producer Shel Talmy. Young decided to stop writing songs with Wright and instead pair off with Vanda,

which turned out to be a masterstroke. Young played Talmy the now-iconic opening chords of 'Friday On My Mind', which was all he had, and the producer told him to go away and work on it. However, Young went to the movies first. A documentary that ran before the movie featured the French vocal act The Swingle Singers, who used a lot of 'doo-doos' and 'daa-daas'. It inspired the Easybeats songwriters to include some in this song they were working on.

'Friday on My Mind', a song inspired by a French group and written in England by a Scot and a Dutchman went to No. 6 in the UK, No. 1 in Australia and even cracked the US *Billboard* charts, reaching No. 16. From there it was all downhill for The Easybeats which, unable to repeat the success of 'Friday On My Mind', struggled on for several years before breaking up in 1969. Vanda and Young recorded a few hits under various names and wrote classics for other artists such as 'Evie' for Stevie Wright and 'Love Is In The Air' for John Paul Young.

Until 'Friday on My Mind', The Easybeats were writing love songs that catered to the teenagers screaming in the front row of their shows or chasing them down the streets. 'Friday' was a song that spoke to their older working-class siblings, who had left school and were doing time on factory assembly lines. For them there was no long view, no career goals to look forward to; the likelihood was that in 10 years they'd still be standing in the same spot on that assembly line. For them the focus was on the end of the week, on Friday, an idea that carried them through the working week. The lyrics for 'Friday On My Mind' tapped into that.

Today, writing songs about waiting for the weekend to come are a bit of a cliché. In The Easybeats' days, when the bulk of songs were about love, 'Friday On My Mind' was something fresh and different and, as George Young saw it, the song didn't champion the workers over the middle class but rather made a veiled comment about the whole situation. 'It's understandable why it can be seen as an ode to the working class given the weekly grind of the average punter,' he said, 'but it has more to do with [our] outlook on the world than any class statement.'

That outlook hasn't changed all that much in the decades since Vanda and Young wrote 'Friday On My Mind': workers still count down the days to the weekend.

CHAPTER 13

Sounds Of Then
(This Is Australia)

★ ★ ★ ★ ★ ★ ★ ★ ★ ★ ★ ★

GANGGAJANG

The part of the title in parentheses wasn't there when GANGgajang recorded this tune for their debut album back in 1985. It was only added later after the song appeared in a Coca-Cola ad and people went to the record store – back when we did such things – asking for a song called 'This Is Australia'. You can't really blame people for doing that: who names a song after a phrase that appears in the first line and then never again?

The idea makes more sense when you realise it was never meant to be a song about Australia. Rather, it was a look back at songwriter Mark Callaghan's youth, when his family migrated from England to Bundaberg when he was aged 14. Hence, it was for him the sounds of *then*, of his *past*. 'It's one of those songs where if your goal was only to sell records, whatever it took to do it, then the song would have been called "This Is Australia",' Callaghan said.

'But it's not about that. It's a brick-veneer drama. My parents got divorced when they came to Australia. It was a horrible period of my life, and the song is actually about how smells and sounds and sensations can rekindle a memory – which is what music does so successfully for people.'

The most-remembered part of the song – sitting on the patio, breathing humidity while watching the lightning crack – was written as a poem by Callaghan when he was 15 and new to the country. The words came out years later when Callaghan, who had been in Brisbane band The Riptides, teamed up with ex-Angels Graham 'Buzz' Bidstrup and Chris Bailey to work on the music for the iconic 1984 ABC TV series *Sweet and Sour*. From there GANGgajang, a name that references the sound of an acoustic guitar being strummed, came about, fleshing out the line-up with Bidstrup's wife Kayellen Bee, Robbie James and Geoffrey Stapleton.

'Sounds Of Then' wasn't a song that jumped out for the band: by the time they released it as a single they'd already put out four other 45s from the album. Even then it wasn't a smash, reaching No. 35 on the charts, but like so many other anthems the song ended up having a life of its own: appearing in the Coke ad, as well as being used by both the Nine and Ten networks as a promotional theme. That was enough to earn the single a rerelease. The song kept on resonating, with a Sarah Blasko version of the song being used in 2021 to flog Colorbond steel. 'I've never had a hit,' Callaghan said, 'but a good number of my songs kind of ooze, continue to ooze.'

The reason this song has continued to ooze is due to what people think it's about. As mentioned in the introduction, there can be a difference between what a songwriter is writing about and how an audience hears it. In the case of 'Sounds Of Then' it's likely almost nobody has listened to the lyrics and realised they are about the divorce of Callaghan's parents – though the fact it became popular meant he had to sing a song

about that touchy subject over and over again. Like plenty of other musicians who have to play the same songs, chances are he went on autopilot when 'Sounds Of Then' appeared on the set list.

What other people hear in the song are distinctly Australian references that make sense no matter where they live. Well, except maybe if they live in Tasmania, because those references are all about the heat of an Aussie summer: the night-time heat, breathing in the humidity if you're outside, lying in bed sweating from the heat of summer if you're inside. The heat reference is right there in the chorus, which is handy because that's the part of the song most people remember – the evocative bit about lightning cracking over cane fields is just another little image of Australia to hang on to. So a song about a kid's parents splitting up turns into an ode to Australia.

SOUNDS OF THEN (THIS IS AUSTRALIA)

For the first few years of Missy Higgins's music career there was almost as much focus on who she liked to sleep with as on the tunes. She broke through when in 2001 she won triple j's Unearthed competition as a teenager, at which age it's hard enough to figure out for yourself who you are and who you like without pesky music journalists trying to trip you up and use a telltale pronoun. 'Every time I did an interview I was in shutdown mode,' she said, 'because they were probing, trying to get me to slip up. Trying to get me to say a pronoun, you know? I'd be like, "How do I describe what this song's about without saying she?"'

What does it matter whether she wrote a song about a guy or a girl? A love song is a love song and a break-up song is a break-up song regardless of who is it about. Knowing it's

about a girl shouldn't change whether or not it's a good song. In fact, it's totally irrelevant to anyone but Higgins herself.

The pointless speculation first came up with her 2004 breakout hit 'Scar'. Incredibly for a debut single from an artist still in her teens it entered the charts at No. 1 and spent 21 weeks in the top 40. Soon after its release people noticed the use of those dreaded pronouns. The first verse was about a 'he' and the second about 'she', both of whom don't seem happy with Higgins as she was and felt she had to change – hence the line about 'cutting me so I'd fit'.

People figured it had to be a song about Higgins's bisexuality, about having her heart broken by a girl and a guy. As recently as 2015 LGBTQI+ magazine *The Advocate* included 'Scar' in a list of pop songs about bisexuality but it's got nothing to do with that: it's about songwriting. When Higgins was working on her debut album *The Sound Of White* her label set up sessions with a number of co-writers to see what might develop. Some of the co-writes were good experiences – 'Scar' itself is the result of a collaboration – but others didn't go quite so well. The lyrics of 'Scar' are about two of those.

At the time Higgins was quite protective of her lyrics, feeling that if the words were hers then the song remained hers as well. Higgins told Linda Marigliano on triple j's Inspired podcast that the 'he' in the first verse was 'an old German pop star from the '80s' who was working on a song with her. She went back to her hotel, wrote all the lyrics and took them back in the next day. 'He said, "I don't really think we can include this line or this line and I think you should change this line to this because 15-year-old girls are not going to be able to relate to this,"' Higgins said. 'I was so humiliated, and I couldn't believe that this guy was trying to dumb down my lyrics.'

The 'she' in the second verse was a female songwriter making tea in the next room while Higgins played a song. Later, that woman put in for a 50 per cent songwriting credit for a song she had little to do with. 'He was trying to squeeze me into this place where everyone else was going just because it would make me more acceptable and more palatable,' Higgins said, 'and she was trying to take advantage of me, I guess. They were two really bad experiences I had, and that's what ended up being the content of the song "Scar."'

The fact people have misconstrued the subject matter of 'Scar' doesn't bother Higgins. She recognises songs can end up with a life of their own once they reach other people's ears. 'I think, to be honest, that's the reason why I don't usually explain exactly who my songs are about or what they're about. I really like the fact that people can interpret it the way they want to. Otherwise it's a very specific song about your own personal experience, and nobody's going to be able to relate to exactly what you've been through.'

CHAPTER 15
Love Is In The Air
JOHN PAUL YOUNG

If you have a hit with one song and need a guaranteed follow-up, why not write another song that sounds pretty much the same? That's what Harry Vanda and George Young did when John Paul Young had an accidental hit in Germany with 'Standing In The Rain' – accidental because the song was on the B-side of the actual single 'Keep On Smilin''. DJs preferred what was on the flipside and played 'Standing In The Rain', making it a hit.

There was a need to strike while the iron was hot, so Vanda and Young essentially sampled the drum loop – it was too hard to get a real drummer to play that basic rhythm all the way through the song – from 'Standing In The Rain' and wrote a new song over the top of it to create 'Love Is In The Air'. 'It's probably the only song I heard and instantly thought, "This has got legs, this might make it,"' John Paul Young said, 'which is testament to George and Harry. It has that certain something. I don't know what it is and I don't even think George and Harry know what it is. If they did, they'd write another one.'

Vanda and Young did know they had something special, because it stood up to repeated listens. 'We put down the demo in the studio and something happened that very seldom happened,' Vanda said. 'We played the bloody thing 20 times on the way home, over and over and over and over, and didn't get sick of it.' They even decided to leave in John Paul Young's 'whoa-whoa', which had been a placeholder where they intended to add some extra words. However, after they listened to it on the way home the pair figured the 'whoa-whoas' worked just fine.

It went top 10 around the world, reaching No. 1 on the *Billboard* adult contemporary charts. It gained a new lease of life in 1992 when an updated version was featured in Baz Lurhmann's hit film *Strictly Ballroom*, which occurred due to a happy coincidence. The film was made by a studio owned by Albert Productions, which also owned the record label that was releasing John Paul Young's songs. With a small film budget Lurhmann couldn't afford to pay to license songs, so taking songs from the Albert catalogue

was the financially wise solution. That's why three JPY songs appear on the movie soundtrack, the other two being 'Standing In The Rain' and 'Yesterday's Hero' – though the latter is sung by former Jimmy and the Boys frontman Ignatius Jones.

In 2020 'Love Is In The Air' became part of a copyright infringement case. Boomerang Investment, which held the copyright to the song, weren't happy that US electronic duo Glass Candy's song 'Warm In The Winter' included the line 'Love is in the air, whoa-whoah', so Boomerang took them to court. They also brought in Air France, which had used a version of the Glass Candy song for a commercial. While Glass Candy denied ever hearing 'Love Is In The Air' the court disagreed, in part because the song was played around Glass Candy sets. It decided the duo had deliberately copied the lines, which were a fundamental part of the original song.

Most of the damages claims were dismissed because Boomerang had targeted the band's making the song available for streaming as an infringement of copyright. The court ruled the Australasian Performing Right Association and not Boomerang held the rights relating to digital streaming.

CHAPTER 16

Am I Ever Gonna See Your Face Again

THE ANGELS

When it comes to the infamous chant that accompanies this song, the one with the swear words, it was an unknown DJ who was responsible. The first time the band heard it was in Mount Isa in 1978 or maybe 1983: the band's members have given different years. 'I was a bit shocked the first time. I didn't know why we were being told to "Fuck off",' singer Doc Neeson said. 'After the show I jumped down into the audience and asked a guy why he was telling me to fuck off. He said they were singing along to the song with the chant that started at a blue light disco. The DJ would stop the song and the crowd would sing the chant.'

The profanity-laden chant doesn't really sit well with the sad origins of the song, because Neeson wrote it about a tragedy that befell their manager John Woodruff. While at university he and his girlfriend left Adelaide to head out to the country for a romantic weekend. She had to be back for lectures on Monday and left early, while Woodruff stayed in the country until Wednesday. 'On Monday night her bike ran into a telegraph pole; she was a motorcycle rider,' Neeson told writer Murray Engleheart. 'John was telling me about it something like eighteen months after that tragedy and he was going through the feeling of: I wonder what happens on the other side? And will we ever meet again? I was really touched by the depth of his emotion. That was where I got the idea: am I ever going to see your face again?'

It explains the iconic riff at the start of the song, which resembles an ambulance siren. The song started life as a ballad before the band changed it into a rock boogie, although they did have a few goes at it: the 1976 single version is faster than what they recorded for their debut album a year later Oddly, they removed the ambulance siren riff when they recorded it for the album.

There was a bit of tension with UK band Status Quo, which noted the song bore an uncanny similarity to their B-side 'Lonely Nights'. They had a point, because if you listen to it, it's hard to refute. Quo bassist Alan Lancaster mentioned it to Angels guitarist John Brewster, who didn't believe him until he played the song to The Angels co-founder. 'So I asked Doc, "Is it possible that you might have ripped off a Status Quo song?" and he replied "Er . . . I might have heard it at a disco." So we did some negotiation: we made them an offer. It was a private arrangement but, yeah, they [Quo] did get a piece of our song.'

The song itself is an odd choice for one of the best-known Angels tunes as it came before they hit upon their signature sound. They needed to find something that would instantly identify an Angels song, and that came with the song 'I Aint The One' from their hit second album of 1978, *Face to Face*. Tagged the 'nik niks', the technique was a rapid nicking of the guitar strings. Also, it may come as a surprise that 'Am I Ever Going To See Your Face Again' wasn't a hit when it was first released. The song didn't break the top 40 in 1976, only managing a best position of No. 58. A 1988 version released in conjunction with the double live album *Liveline* did much better, reaching No. 11.

120   AUSSIE ROCK ANTHEMS

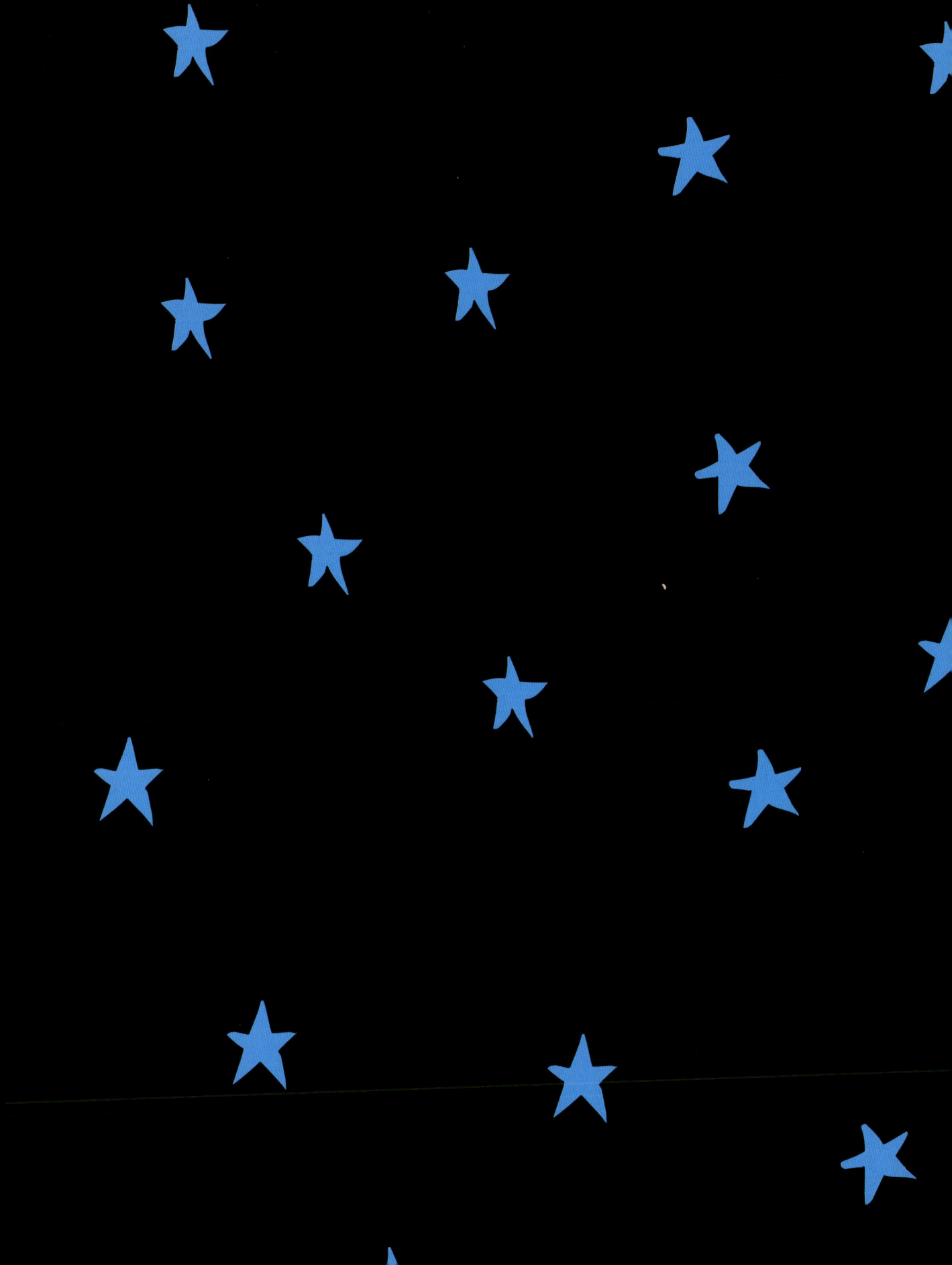

CHAPTER 17
BERLIN CHAIR
YOU AM I

★ ★ ★ ★ ★ ★ ★ ★ ★ ★

Eggs? Why is frontman Tim Rogers singing about eggs? There's a line in this song where he sings he'll 'give all my eggs to you', which comes across as the strangest, most opaque part of the song. The reality is Rogers says 'aches', not 'eggs', although even though you know that it's still hard not to hear 'eggs' whenever you listen to this song. You can go online and find forums where people get very into the 'eggs/aches' argument. It even features as a dramatic plot point in Tim Minchin's TV series *Upright*, where 13-year-old Meg is trying to decipher the lyric while driving along the Nullarbor. As the ghost of her brother who took his own life appears beside her, Meg has the tear-laded realisation that the word is 'aches'.

Rogers wrote the song when he was living in the Sydney suburb of Chippendale, but said he didn't remember recording it for the album. It was only when bassist Andy Kent told him on the flight back from the US, where the album was recorded, that 'Berlin Chair' should be the first single.

It didn't end up as the first single: it was the second, released in February 1994, but Kent was right to think there was something special about 'Berlin Chair'. While it didn't do anything special on the charts, reaching no higher than No. 73, it became one of You Am I's most iconic songs. Triple j listeners voted it the top Australian song of the 1990s in a phone poll, while Budweiser liked the song enough to want to use it on a US radio ad. After much to-ing and fro-ing the band said 'No,' to the annoyance of their American label.

Part of the reason 'Berlin Chair' has hung around is because it harkens back to the early 1990s, which was the heyday for You Am I so there's an element of nostalgia going on. It would have been the song that turned many people on to You Am I. Yes, they had plenty of other songs, but fans always remember the first time they heard a band and fell in love with them.

There's also a lot going on in the lyrics, and lyrics are something hardcore fans go

over with a fine-toothed comb. The lyrics see Rogers wearing his heart on his sleeve, begging someone to stay with him while at the same time identifying all his own flaws. Maybe it's not the first time the narrator has screwed up, given he's 'the re-run you'll always force yourself to sit through'. When you put that fine-toothed comb over the lyrics it seems to be about an imploding relationship, one that has run its course but the participants feel on some level that perhaps it's better to be in an ordinary partnership than none at all. At its core, 'Berlin Chair' is a break-up song albeit one with sublime lyrics emotionally delivered and a brilliantly simple guitar riff.

The video for 'Berlin Chair' stood out thanks to the work of an old boxer named PJ. Dressed in a sparkly silver jumpsuit, he does an odd yet endearing stutter-shake dance routine that everyone remembers.

The US label didn't think much of it, and made them shoot a different version in which the band members are dressed in suits like a 1960s pop band performing on a TV show. It's not as good as the version with PJ, although the band does look sharp in those suits.

In case you're wondering, a Berlin chair is a real thing. It was created in 1923 by furniture designer Gerrit Rietveld for a Berlin exhibition, and Rogers saw it in a Canberra exhibition and kept the name to use as a song title. Made of eight separate panels of solid oak, the chair is lacquered in white, black and grey. With an armrest on one side and a vertical panel of wood on the other, it looks like a distinctly uncomfortable chair – one sure to give you a few aches. If you want to buy one, copies are available; you just need more than $4000 to blow on a chair you can't sit on.

BERLIN CHAIR 125

CHAPTER 18

Don't Dream It's Over

CROWDED HOUSE

This song is viewed as being one of Crowded House's best, but back in 1986 when it was released the band had to literally buy its way into the US charts. There was no problem with the self-titled debut album or any of its singles cracking the charts in Australia and New Zealand: due to the strong fanbase built up from Neil Finn's time in Split Enz, the album reached No. 1 in Australia and No. 3 in the Shaky Isles. The first three singles from the album also made the top 40.

'Don't Dream It's Over', the fourth single spun off from the album, went top 10 in New Zealand and Australia, but in the United States the band's label Capitol Records quickly lost interest in promoting them to radio. The early singles didn't spark much airplay, and the bods at Capitol went cold on Crowded House. 'About three months into the release of the album,' manager Gary Stamler told biographer Chris Bourke, 'the climate in the record company – beyond a few real believers – was that there were lots of problems with the record.'

In 1986 the media exposed the world of the independent promoters and their links to the Mafia. In response the major labels decided to boycott the promoters, both as an attempt to look clean and also rid themselves of the high fees.

Stamler decided on a slightly sneaky plan. In the US music industry was a group of people known as independent promoters, who were hired by labels at exorbitant fees to get singles played on the radio. Most commonly this was done through the means of bribes, aka payola, with the labels hiring the promoters to keep themselves at arm's length from the shadowy practice.

Months after the release of 'Don't Dream It's Over' only a few stations in the US were playing it, so Stamler – without the knowledge of almost everyone at Capitol – engaged four promoters at a cost of US$10,000, a fraction of what they used to get paid, to work their magic on the Crowded House tune. It succeeded: bigger radio stations started spinning it, which led

128   AUSSIE ROCK ANTHEMS

to MTV playing the video to viewers across the country. The song made it all the way to No. 2 on the *Billboard* charts. Stamler later said that while Capitol was supportive of the band, the promoters were needed to give the song a much-needed nudge.

The band itself was founded in 1985 after Finn left Split Enz and took drummer Paul Hester with him. They filled out their line-up with bassist Nick Seymour, the brother of Mark from Hunters & Collectors, though at the time they were known as The Mullanes. Capitol wanted a name change before the first album was released, their preference being 'Neil Finn and the [insert name here]', which no one in the band liked. After a lot of thought they opted to use the name they had given to the debut album: Crowded House.

Finn wrote 'Don't Dream It's Over' while he and Hester were staying in brother Tim's house in Melbourne. One night some of Hester's friends came round and Finn didn't feel like talking to them, so he shut himself off in a room and less than an hour later there was the song.

In 1996, when the band decided to call it a day, they played their last gig outside the Sydney Opera House on 24 November. Fittingly, 'Don't Dream It's Over' was the last song they played that night. Watching footage of that final song, there is plenty of emotion onstage and especially from Hester, who plays the song while trying to hold back tears. Plenty of people standing on the Opera House steps that night were feeling very much the same. ☀

DON'T DREAM IT'S OVER

CHAPTER 19

I Was Only 19

(A Walk In The Light Green)

REDGUM

Although Frankie has been immortalised in this song he's never kicked any mine the day mankind kicked the moon, but he is a real person. Frankie Hunt was there in the jungle on the morning of 21 July with his platoon, part of 6 Battalion. They'd been away from their base at Nui Dat for a week, and that morning they were sent to check out a deserted village near a mined area.

After slogging through the jungle, the platoon took a break. Commander Peter Hines walked over to speak with the platoon medic, then he turned around and stepped over some packs and onto an M16 Jumping Jack mine. 'A thick black cloud of greyish-brown jungle dirt surged 20 metres into the sticky humid air,' Steve Strevens wrote in his book about Frankie Hunt, 'while sticks and leaves and rubble floated down through the dust. Jagged shrapnel sliced through the air and tore into the soft, sweaty flesh of nearly all the men.'

The explosion killed Hines and wounded 18 men, including Frankie, whose left leg was shattered and whose face, arm and chest were left burning with shrapnel wounds. While Hunt survived the landmine blast, he was in hospital for two years. He went through 30 operations but still had pieces of shrapnel and mashed-up bone floating around in his body. The physical pain was so bad he later told his psychiatrist that, since the injury, there were maybe two days when he hadn't been in pain. There was also the mental and emotional pain: suffering from post-traumatic stress disorder, there were times he would lock the front door of his Bega home and leave a note on it asking people not to knock.

Songwriter John Schumann wrote 'I Was Only 19' in 1983 based on the experiences of his brother-in-law Mick Storen, who was on patrol with Frankie that fateful day.

Schumann felt the lives of Vietnam soldiers could have easily been his own – it could have been his birthday that had been pulled out of the draft lottery – so it was a case of 'There but for the grace of God go I.' He also noted what happened when the soldiers returned to Australia. 'They came home to a bitterly divided society. A lot of people in their naivety and blindness blamed these poor young people for the sins of their respective governments,' Schumann said. 'These kids came home sick, confused and puzzled at the sense that their nation wasn't [as] grateful as the nation was grateful to their fathers.'

He was inspired to write a song about their struggle but didn't want to base it on his imagination or news reports he'd seen – which was where Storen came in. Schumann asked if he could talk about his experiences and Storen said 'Yes', so they sat together and talked. Schumann recorded everything on 90-minute cassette tapes; By the end he had nine of those tapes. He listened to the tapes for months without writing a word or a chord, until he sat in the backyard of his Carlton house. 'I put my guitar on my lap.

Schumann had married Storen's sister Denise; she is the 'Denny' referred to in the first line of the song.

In the song it was initially a fictional 'Tommy' who kicked the mine, though Storen told Schumann he didn't know anyone named Tommy while in the army. While 'Peter' did fit, they decided Hines's family didn't need constant reminders of what had happened every time they heard the song. The name Frankie fit, so he was included in the song, although only after seeking Hunt's approval.

AUSSIE ROCK ANTHEMS

I hadn't written a line, I hadn't written a note before this, I just had this conversation playing in my head for months and months and months,' he said. 'I wrote "I Was Only 19", and the very strange thing is I've still got the original, and there are very few changes and edits on it at all. It's almost as if it had [already] been written. And as proud as I am of having written that song, you know, that morning I felt little more than a conduit.'

Part of the deal with Storen was that he had to hear it first, and if he didn't like it the song wouldn't see the light of day. Once he heard it Storen directed him to Frankie down in Bega, who was so touched by the song he kept asking Schumann to play it again. So many other veterans since have been touched by the fact someone had presented their case to their country, though at gigs they left the room when Schumann played it because of the pain it brought up.

The song also helped to tell the veterans' stories to Australia as a whole, making them realise what these soldiers had gone through and what they still go through. 'I think "I Was Only 19" provides an "I get it" moment,' Schumann said. 'Australians are fundamentally fair and decent, and I think "I Was Only 19" was a story . . . that made us stop and think, "Oh, shit, we didn't do the right thing by those blokes." It gave us all a chance to look over the fence, and look into the backyards of the Vietnam veterans who lived next door or down the street.'

The song was Redgum's biggest hit, reaching No. 1 and going platinum three times. Technically, it wasn't a Redgum song at all. Redgum songwriter Michael Atkinson told Schumann the band didn't want to record it as a single because they'd done that a few times before with his songs and they hadn't sold, so he went off and recorded it on his own with the help of Redgum violinist Hugh McDonald, and released it under the band's name because it had some traction.

It has become part of the Midnight Oil lore that they never appeared on *Countdown*, though the truth is they were willing to do so early in their career but a last-minute hiccup stopped it from happening. Redgum, at least during Schumann's tenure in the band, also never appeared on the popular ABC Sunday night show – not even when they had a No. 1 single with 'I Was Only 19'.

'When "I Was Only 19" was No. 1 the producers of *Countdown* asked me to bring the band on to the program,' Schumann remembered. 'In keeping with our position at the time, I refused. They then asked to show our clip. I refused permission as our clip featured me and my position was that we were not to appear on *Countdown*, either live or on film. *Countdown* cut its own clip without me in it.' Two years after Schumann left Redgum did perform live on *Countdown*, performing the song 'Roll It On Robbie', a cringeworthy tune that unfortunately became the last thing ever heard from the band.

I WAS ONLY 19 (A WALK IN THE LIGHT GREEN)

CHAPTER 20

GET FREE

THE VINES

The music media's tendency to pour the hype on thick is hard for any band to deal with. There's huge pressure with everyone labelling you the 'next big thing', and what so often follows is a pile-on as the band is criticised for not living up to their potential – never mind the fact it was the media and not the band that decided what that potential was in the first place. The media can't be stupid, so it must have been the band's fault, and it's so much worse when your lead singer and songwriter has an undiagnosed mental health condition.

Such was the case with The Vines, which started out as Rishikesh in Sydney in 1994 before changing their name. By 2001 The Vines hadn't really established any profile in Australia, then in November of that year their debut single 'Factory' was released in the UK and the hype began. *NME* magazine named it single of the week, doing the same in March 2002 with 'Highly Evolved'. This was all before the band had released anything in Australia.

The debut album *Highly Evolved* came out in July, and in October The Vines were on the cover of the US *Rolling Stone*. The last Australian band to achieve that was Men at Work, but they had to win a Grammy first. Realistically, The Vines had done almost nothing yet. Much of the coverage of the band focused on the antics of frontman Craig Nicholls, joking about how he was insane and mental. During a US tour in 2002 the band appeared on David Letterman's show. Halfway through the song Nicholls missed chords and slurred the lyrics, and at the end of the song he flung his guitar at the drumkit, narrowly missing drummer Hamish Rosser.

The wild ride of The Vines in their most popular form effectively ended on 27 May 2004, with a gig at the Annandale Hotel. Nicholls booted a photographer's camera during the first song, and then three tunes later he abused bassist Patrick Matthews so badly he left the stage, jumped in a taxi and never returned. The confrontation with *Sun-Herald* photographer Janie Barrett saw Nicholls charged with assault, a charge that was dismissed when he appeared in court in November that year because, since the assault, Nicholls had been diagnosed with Asperger's syndrome. 'The guy who diagnosed Craig,' Vines co-manager Andy Kelly stated, 'said his life consisted pretty much of the worst things you could do for someone in his condition: being in a different place every day, meeting new people, just having everything be totally unstructured. Things went downhill very quickly'.

With the benefit of hindsight, a lot of the signs were there. Nicholls had a strong preference for food from McDonald's, which tastes the same all over the world, felt better in the studio than on the road and was noticeably uncomfortable in crowded backstage areas after shows. 'When they got to the UK and Europe it started getting hard again, really hard,' co-manager Andy Cassell said, 'and by the time the Annandale show happened we realised he couldn't handle the stress anymore.' Since that time The Vines has become a vehicle for Nicholls's songs, backed by various other members. Following the debut album he put out six other releases and plays live on a very limited schedule.

The Vines will always be remembered for 'Get Free', a short song at just 2.06 minutes by modern standards but one that doesn't waste a second of that time. That's to the song's benefit: it doesn't outstay its welcome and is in fact over too soon, leaving you with the urge to hear it again. What's it about? Your guess is as good as mine: something about taking a photo, driving around a corner and moving out of California, followed by getting free from something.

AUSSIE ROCK ANTHEMS

There's not really anything deep going on in those lyrics, as though Nicholls came up with some placeholder lines and never got around to changing them to anything better.

However, it doesn't matter because sometimes the lyrics just don't matter and they're certainly never the first thing that grab you about a song. No one dances to words, they dance to music, which is where 'Get Free' makes its statement. There's the killer riff that opens the song, which stamped it as being something different from all the other stuff that was on the radio. Nicholls plays on the wild riff by delivering his lines in what can only be described as a howl that likely shredded his vocal cords during the recording. The busy drumming of session muso Joey Waronker (it might be band member Rosser in the video but it's not him drumming on the song; the things you learn by reading the liner notes) add to the frenetic garage-rock feel of the song. It's as though they're all racing each other to get to the end of the song first. The result is a blast of loud, crazy, about to run off the rails rock.

It's no surprise 'Get Free' is far and away The Vines's most popular song on Spotify. At the time of writing it was approaching 80 million plays, and there's a gap of 70 million plays to their second-most popular song.

GET FREE 137

CHAPTER 21

Are You Gonna Be My Girl

JET

Like The Vines, Jet got caught up in a hype machine, the big difference being that the Melbourne band craved the attention. The four-piece's rise was steeper than that of The Vines: Jet formed in 2001, and by 2003 their debut 'Get Born' was charting all over the world. Things got even crazier when 'Are You Gonna Be My Girl', which had reportedly been written by frontman Nic Cester while he was on the toilet, featured in ads for Apple's iPod. With hindsight, landing the iPod ad seems like it would have been a big deal, but this was 2003 and the iPod was an unknown quantity.

'We had no idea what it was,' Cester said, 'but we could tell by the way the managers and the label were talking that it was a big deal. We did "Umm" and "Ahh" about it because back then, while we didn't know what an iPod was, if you allowed your music to be used on any commercial you ran the risk of getting crucified.'

While they never got a free iPod out of the deal, Jet did get truckloads of exposure. It was a massive help in the US, where

'Get Born' had been out for more than six months but was not getting much traction. 'That was definitely a tipping point,' Cester said of the ad. 'That kind of global exposure is game changing definitely, particularly then with the iPod because it was *the* new product that everyone was talking about.'

It's a damned catchy song with a great groove, which helps it stick in listeners' heads. Also, it doesn't hurt that it sounds like a few other songs so it rides on the coat-tails of that familiarity. There are clear hallmarks of Iggy Pop's 'Lust For Life', The Jam's 'A Town Called Malice' and even The Supremes's 'You Can't Hurry Love'. 'I've always accepted the comparison [with 'Lust For Life'], it's true,' Cester told *VICE Magazine*. 'I would say our song is just another in a long line of songs with that rhythm.'

Part of the song that is definitely unique is Cester's cough just before he delivers his first line. The cough was part of the original demo for the song, which they recorded in Melbourne. While it was an accidental cough, the band became so attached to it that they took the cough from the demo and added it to the LA album recording.

'Are You Gonna Be My Girl' hit the top spot in the 2003 triple j Hottest 100. It went to No. 16 in the UK and No. 29 in the US, and the album *Get Born* did similar business. However, as is the nature of a band that experiences a sudden massive rise in popularity, Jet couldn't sustain the momentum. Their follow-up album *Shine On* may have charted

better in the UK and US but it fell out of those charts even faster. Some of the reviews indicated that Jet's take on rock was wearing thin: giving it a rating of 0, Ray Suzuki's review on the Pitchfork website consisted of nothing more than a video of a monkey urinating in its own mouth.

In 2009 came the band's third album *Shaka Rock*, which didn't set the world on fire despite Jet's efforts to tour the bejesus out of it. It was clear that Jet's time had come and gone: they'd become a nostalgia act before they even broke up, with audiences only wanting to hear stuff from their first album. In 2012 the inevitable happened and the band split up, but it's not bad to be able to leave a legacy such as 'Are You Gonna Be My Girl'.

CHAPTER 22

Great Southern Land

ICEHOUSE

'Whatever you do, don't say it's about Australia.'

That was the advice songwriter Iva Davies's manager gave him when this song was released in 1982. At the time, before *Crocodile Dundee* made Australia the flavour of the month everywhere, Australian acts were expected to have an international flavour rather than singing about their own country. 'The Australian cultural cringe was a thing back then,' Davies said. 'My manager wanted Icehouse to be perceived as an international band, not just an Australian band, and the last thing he wanted me to do was talk about it being a song about Australia. It was so obvious it was a song about Australia. He said to suggest maybe it was about Antarctica or South Africa or some imaginary place.'

Davies just couldn't do it. Understandable, given the inspiration for the song came when he was literally looking at Australia. He was on a flight to London for the band's first international tour, staring out the window at the expanse of red dirt and scrub below. He fell asleep, woke up two hours later and the view out the window hadn't changed. 'I'd been flying for two hours over the red centre of Australia and it was only in that moment that the sheer vast scale of the continent dawned on me,' Davies said.

'Great Southern Land' came at the perfect time for Davies: the extended tour of Europe for Icehouse, formerly known as Flowers, gave him an extreme sense of homesickness followed by a nervous breakdown. That led to him breaking up the band, but there was still an international record deal that demanded another album. That and the debts racked up by touring fell on Davies's shoulders, so he had to crank out some material for what would become the album *Primitive Man*.

The first song he wrote was 'Great Southern Land', and he used an unusual method to come up with the lyrics. He took inspiration from writer William S. Burroughs's cut-up method, which involved combining unrelated words written on pieces of paper. 'I literally cut the pieces of paper and put them down on the floor and shuffled

144 AUSSIE ROCK ANTHEMS

them around in three-word phrases,' Davies said. 'Instead of trying to write a cohesive but ultimately unsatisfactory narrative about Australia, I simply just served up a palette of colours really.'

There was some resistance from the label when they heard the song, and not just because it was about Australia. 'Great Southern Land' clocks in at five minutes and 15 seconds, which was much longer than the three-minute pop songs radio preferred to play. There was talk about cutting off the long synth intro, anything to reduce the length of the song, but Davies stood his ground.

It turned out he was right. The song went to No. 5 in Australia and appeared on the soundtrack for the Yahoo Serious film *Young Einstein*. It made the National Film and Sound Archive of Australia's Sounds of Australia list, reserved for pieces that have cultural or historical significance to Australia. (Also on the list are 'You're The Voice', INXS's 'Don't Change', Hilltop Hoods's 'Nosebleed Section' and Kevin Rudd's apology to the Stolen Generation.) In 2017 when Qantas introduced the first of eight Boeing 787-9 Dreamliners to the fleet it was named Great Southern Land.

Even without knowing that Davies's inspiration for the song came from looking out at the Australian landscape through the window of an airplane, you can hear it in the music: there's an atmospheric, soundtrack-like feel that comes from the synthesizers combined with the space within the music replicating the vast emptiness of the outback. The lyrics, created by that cut-and-paste approach, convey an impressionist picture that gives listeners enough of an image to know it's about Australia thanks to phrases such as a 'prisoner island' and oblique references to First Nations people. However, it's an incomplete image, one that allows the listener to fill in their own meaning. ✹

CHAPTER 23

HORROR MOVIE

SKYHOOKS

'Horror Movie' was one of just two singles released from Skyhooks's 1974 debut album *Livin' In The 70's*, the other being the title track. One likely reason these two songs were released as singles was because they were pretty much the only songs that weren't banned from the radio.

The Federation of Australian Radio Broadcasters was so outraged by the contents of the album they slapped a ban on six of the 10 songs. Songs such as 'Toorak Cowboy', 'Smut', 'Motorcycle Bitch', 'Hey, What's The Matter' and 'You Just Like Me Cos I'm Good In Bed' had the red line drawn through them for their references to drugs and sex. Most of the references were pretty tame, such as the offending line in 'Toorak Cowboy' being about buying a matchbox of dope, and show that the early 1970s in Australia were in some ways a repressed time. To nail their colours to the mast, when Double J started in 1975 the first song they played was 'You Just Like Me Cos I'm Good In Bed'.

Michael Gudinski, the boss of Skyhooks's Mushroom Records label, was far from upset about the ban. To him it was a great marketing gimmick. 'I think one of the biggest things that helped them at the time, and it was a stroke of genius . . . When all the songs got banned, I thought, "This is fantastic. If they want the record, they're going to have to buy it, they're not going to hear it all over the radio."'

It was the 'Horror Movie' single that broke the band and created Skyhooks mania. The album's title track was released in August, two months ahead of the long player, but only received sporadic airplay. There was nothing there that hinted that Mushroom had a huge band on their hands. That changed with the January 1975 release of 'Horror Movie', which went to No. 1 and became the band's signature track. 'I think one week it went from 34 to six on the charts,' Gudinski said. 'That was when I knew. You can't have records jump like that, you can't hype, you can't push. When it moves like that it's the real thing. It all just happened so fast.'

At the time the *Livin' In The 70's* album was released Mushroom Records was, financially speaking, living on the edge and Gudinski needed some hits to generate cash flow. The album saved the label, going to No. 1 and selling 200,000 copies, a record for an Australian artist at the time.

One of the lasting legacies of Skyhooks was that they broke down the cultural cringe, showing bands they could write about Australia and be successful. 'Horror Movie' was actually one of the few songs on the album that didn't reference a Melbourne suburb and perhaps that led to a broader appeal, given people outside of Melbourne in the 1970s might not get the in-jokes attached to references to suburbs such as Balwyn, Carlton or Toorak. 'Horror Movie' focuses on the mad state of the world; the lyrics suggest the song is about watching a scary film with car crashes, police brutality and teens brawling in the streets. It's only at the end that the zinger comes: it's not a movie but the nightly news. There's also a dig at TV stations for cashing in on people's urge to see view real-life horrors.

Most of the album was written by bassist Greg Macainsh and it was he who was responsible for name dropping suburbs, though he's the first to admit it wasn't a conscious decision to write about Melbourne rather than New York. 'I didn't really know what I was doing back then,' he said. 'It just made sense for me to write about the things I knew. The only other "Australian" song I knew at the time was "I've Been Everywhere", which had every Oodnadatta/Coolangatta/Wangaratta rhyme. It was a novelty song and I definitely didn't want to go in that direction.'

AUSSIE ROCK ANTHEMS

CHAPTER 24

My Happiness

POWDERFINGER

★ ★ ★ ★ ★ ★ ★ ★ ★

Like a number of other songs in this book, 'My Happiness' offers conclusive proof that people don't really pay attention to lyrics. The song title is "My Happiness" so it must be a love song,' they think, but a cursory reading of the lyrics will show that isn't the case at all. Even if someone just reads the chorus, which details a person's happiness slowly coming back now someone has returned home only to have them pack up and go by the end, it should be a bit of a giveaway.

Rather than being a love song it is about the lack of love that comes when someone is not there. 'It's a sad story of touring and the absence and loneliness that goes with it,' explains the booklet in the band's greatest-hit collection album *Fingerprints*, 'but is mystifyingly thought of as a romantic song.'

The song comes from the band's 2000 album *Odyssey Number Five* and came as a bit of relief. Powderfinger had broken through big time with the preceding album *Internationalist*, which had gone to No. 1 and spent almost two years in the top 50.

The pressure was on for the follow-up, and when the band worked up 'My Happiness' they took it as a sign they were on the right track. Frontman Bernard Fanning remembered the song took some time to come together: 'Recording that song took quite a while. We did a few different tempos. We got maybe halfway through and it was not right, the tempo was too slow.'

They obviously found the right tempo, because the song was the first single from *Odyssey Number Five* and became Powderfinger's best-performing single. It went to No. 4 in Australia and No. 23 on the *Billboard* Modern Rock Tracks and won the ARIA for Single of the Year. It also took out top spot in the triple j Hottest 100 in 2000. Incidentally, *Odyssey Number Five* contained two songs that finished No. 1 in the Hottest 100. A year earlier the Powderfinger tune 'These Days', written for the Heath Ledger film *Two Hands*, reached that spot despite the band only releasing it as a B-side.

The popularity of the song in Australia partly flowed from the misunderstanding of the subject matter. Because it was called

'My Happiness' some felt it was an upbeat song, while others took it to be about a happy reunion of a lover who has returned home. As we've seen it's not really about that at all, but that doesn't matter to the listener. Music is sticky, allowing people to attach whatever meanings they want to a song. If they decide it's a happy song, then it's a happy song. It doesn't hurt that the song does the old trick of lifting the tempo and volume when the chorus kicks in, the chorus being the part of the song people remember most strongly. Also, raising the volume helps to bring it to your attention.

'My Happiness' looked like the song that was going to break the band in the United States. As part of a push over there they played on the *Late Show with David Letterman*. 'It was a bit of a disaster,' Fanning remembered. 'We didn't really nail it. We were so nervous and it was fucking freezing in the studio.' Despite their efforts the US market wouldn't take to it. 'The song just didn't react with the public,' manager Paul Piticco said. 'It was the number one most-added song on radio, in the top 10 most-played song for a couple of weeks and it still didn't sell.'

At least back home in Australia Powderfinger remained kings. The band's next three albums all went to No. 1 in the charts before they called it a day in 2010.

MY HAPPINESS   153

CHAPTER 25

EAGLE ROCK

DADDY COOL

If things had panned out differently, Australians might have been doing the pigeon wing instead of the eagle rock. The song 'Eagle Rock' was Daddy Cool's debut single in 1971, and it sat at No. 1 for what was then a record 10 weeks and also went gold. It was written by frontman Ross Wilson while in England in the late 1960s. When he returned to Australia in the 1970s he formed a band with the awful name Sons Of The Vegetal Mother. Luckily for them they started a side project a year later that went by the name Daddy Cool, and one of their most popular songs was the tune Wilson had brought back from England.

'I was trying to teach myself to play guitar,' Wilson remembered about writing 'Eagle Rock'. 'I used to write a bit on the guitar but I would just strum away pretty badly. I developed the fingerpicking style . . . and then I came up with the riff, which I played for days over and over.'

He played the riff to almost everyone who came to his place because he liked it so much he was convinced he'd subconsciously ripped it off from someone else. He was hoping the people listening might recognise the original song but no one did, suggesting the riff came from Wilson's head. When it came to the words, Wilson said he found inspiration in the pages of the *Sunday Times* newspaper. 'There was a lift-out magazine that had an article on the evolution of American music,' Wilson said. 'The photo showed people dancing at a juke joint. The caption said: "Some [Blacks] doing the eagle rock and cutting the pigeon wing." I'd heard of the pigeon wing but not the eagle rock, and I thought "Wow, what a great name for a dance."'

The eagle rock dance surfaced in the late 1800s before dying out in the 1920s. According to one source, the name came from Kansas City's Eagle Rock Baptist Church, where the congregation moved in a trance-like fashion. The dance itself sees arms stretched out like bird's wings while rocking from side to side with legs close together at the knees.

In the 1970s the Melbourne movement of the Sharpies developed their own dance for

'Eagle Rock', which has been immortalised in video of the 1975 concert for Bangladesh at the Myer Music Bowl; you can check it out on YouTube. It involves bending over and violently thrusting bent arms around, though there is a school of thought that states the sharpies were actually taking the piss when dancing to Daddy Cool playing 'Eagle Rock' because by 1975 the band was decidedly uncool.

In the 1990s a stranger dance arose linked to this song: it was tagged the 'Eagle Drop'. Basically, when the song comes on a group of men stand in a circle and drop their pants. Wilson found out about it around that time while reading a court report in the newspaper. 'I looked down at one of the pages and there was a story that said, "Soldiers fined for lewd behaviour,"' he said. 'I thought it sounded interesting, so I read on. It was datelined Townsville and it read: "Two soldiers were fined for lewd behaviour blah blah blah."' Apparently, in their defence the soldiers told the magistrate they always dropped their pants when 'Eagle Rock' was played!

Why do men do this? No one really seems to know though there are several groups, including footy clubs and military colleges, that have claimed to be the first to do the Eagle Drop. Wilson said it was so ubiquitous at the University of Queensland that the rules in one of their function halls specifically mentioned 'Eagle Rock'. 'There were all the usual rules: no swearing, that kind of thing. Well, you get to number eight and it says: "Patrons will not be ejected by security if they drop their pants during the playing of the song 'Eagle Rock'." Then rule number nine says: "They must pull their pants up when the song is finished."'

CHAPTER 26

April Sun In CUBA

DRAGON

It turns out April may not be the best month to visit Cuba, not if you want to catch the sun. That month is the very tail end of the warmer months, with the wet season coming in May, so if you want to avoid any rain then perhaps go a little earlier than April.

It took Dragon five years to think about that April sun. The band formed in New Zealand in 1972 and established itself on the live circuit, but couldn't translate that popularity to sales of its first two albums. In 1975 the band relocated to Sydney after dismissing initial thoughts of heading to Canada. Soon after they cajoled keyboard player Paul Hewson to fly from New Zealand to join the band, which proved to be a masterstroke: Hewson was the man solely or in part responsible for the band's biggest hits.

'April Sun In Cuba', released in late 1977, was a co-write with singer Marc Hunter, though Hewson got the ball rolling. 'I don't play guitar that much but I was strumming away one day and came up with this feel and Marc wandered into the room,' Hewson said. 'He got his pen out and started scratching away. The sun was streaming into the room and we just thought of Cuba, and we knew we had to get out of [the] hotel room.'

The band was known to be trailed by tragedy: original drummer Neil Storey died of a heroin overdose in 1976, and Hewson

followed the same path in 1985. Even the recording of 'April Sun In Cuba' was tinged with drama, because shortly before doing so Hewson and guitarist Robert Taylor had been in a serious car accident. They'd got into a car to head off for dinner, and the girl behind the wheel ended up putting the car under the wheels of a truck.

Bassist Todd Hunter, who had decided to catch a taxi that night, remembered being in the studio with a few banged-up members. 'When we were recording the backing track, I distinctly remember looking around the studio and thinking we were a bunch of bedraggled, bandaged and neck-braced casualties recording this bright and shiny pop song. I think that more of less sums up the '70s for us.' The bassist also said that situation 'typifies the Dragon story, really. Tragedy but smiling through clenched teeth.'

'April Sun In Cuba' was a big hit for Dragon, going to No. 2 on the Australian charts. It took something like Paul McCartney's 'Mull Of Kintyre' to hold it from the top spot. It became the band's signature song, so much so that a prime minister staring down the barrel of major unpopularity used it to try to win some votes. In 2022 the song hit the headlines when Scott Morrison foolishly tried to play it on the ukulele during a *60 Minutes* profile. Foolishly, because all it did was remind people of the time he buggered off to Hawaii while Australia burned. When he pulled out the uke the *60 Minutes* crew must have been licking their lips, while his minders would have opted for the facepalm.

The band released a caustic statement calling it 'a cynical move for a politician to co-opt music in an attempt to humanise themselves come election time. Maybe if his trip to Hawaii had not been cut short, he could have learn[ed] the lyrics to the rest of the chorus,' the band's statement said.

The song has been the source of a long-running mondegreen, or mishearing of the lyrics. Many people are convinced there is a line that goes 'snake eyes on a pair of dice', when the line as listed on the album lyric sheet reads 'snake eyes on the paradise'. It's a play on words, using something that sounds similar to 'pair of dice' – which obviously makes more sense – to refer to the apparent paradise of Cuba in the month of April.

CHAPTER 27

TOMORROW

SILVERCHAIR

★ ★ ★ ★ ★ ★ ★ ★ ★

It seems that not everyone was able to hear the huge potential in this young Newcastle trio. Back when they were still known as the Innocent Criminals, Daniel Johns, Ben Gillies and Chris Joannou played their first gig at a local street fair. One *Newcastle Herald* letter writer didn't appreciate their noise at all. 'They were absolutely dreadful,' they wrote. 'The music was amplified, it was loud and it was really bad.' However, in a short space of time their abrasive music stormed the international charts.

Johns and Gillies had known each other since primary school and had even formed a rap outfit called the Silly Men. Joannou came on board later, after the Innocent Criminals were up and running and the band realised a bass was an essential component of a rock act – and Joannou's dad had a bass guitar.

In late 1993 the band was invited to record a few songs in a studio at a bargain rate. One of the songs they put down was 'Tomorrow', which had started out as a jam in Gillies's bedroom. Johns had come up with the riff for the song but had to be convinced by Gillies and Joannou that it was worth making into a song. Johns later said the inspiration for the lyrics came from a TV show he had seen. 'There was this poor guy taking a rich guy through a hotel to experience the lot of the less fortunate than him,' Johns said. 'The rich guy is just complaining because he just wants to get out and the poor guy is saying you have to wait 'til tomorrow to get out.'

Several months later a neighbour of the Johns family noticed the SBS program *Nomad* was running a competition called Pick Me for unsigned artists. The trio submitted the tapes from their studio session along with the required 25 words or less about what made the band special: 'We're not hip-hop or rap. We're rock!'

They ended up winning, though the contest organisers were surprised the trio was still in high school. When one rang Johns's house they spoke to his mum but figured she was his wife or girlfriend. Part of the prize was a chance to record at triple j in Sydney, where the six-minute long 'Tomorrow' was cut down to a more radio-friendly length. The band also headed to Newcastle Gaol to shoot a video. By the time the video premiered the band had decided to change its name, feeling that the Innocent Criminals was a bit of a kids' name. From then on they were known as Silverchair.

'Tomorrow' was released in September 1994 and went to No. 1 in Australia and New Zealand. With the flavour of grunge still hanging around and Johns looking uncannily like Kurt Cobain, the song did well overseas too, reaching No. 1 on *Billboard*'s Modern Rock Tracks chart. It also appeared on the band's debut album *Frogstomp*, released in March 1995. The album was a hit in Australia, going six times platinum and making the top 10 on the US *Billboard* charts. *Frogstomp* was the start of a huge run of success for the band, with each of Silverchair's five albums occupying the No. 1 spot. Despite the success of the 'Tomorrow' Johns was always uneasy about it. When Silverchair broke up he was relieved he would never have to play

it again, and it's easy to understand why. Most musicians don't break through until their 20s, when their songwriting has had time to develop. While some write songs in their teens, they're often not proud of them and they have the advantage of nobody hearing them. Not so Johns. He had to deal with millions of people having bought early Silverchair albums, which were full of the songs he wrote as he was developing his craft. It's perhaps something that played into his decision to walk away from the band, as a means to not have to play those songs anymore.

CHAPTER 28

SOLID ROCK

GOANNA

Songwriter Shane Howard and the rest of Goanna pushed for 'Solid Rock' to be the first single from their debut album *Spirit Of Place* despite his belief it would never get commercial airplay, a crucial factor for record companies. He had a point: it's not as though commercial radio in the early 1980s was the sort of place where you'd hear a song that mentioned the word 'genocide'.

However, it did have a solid beat and a catchy guitar riff, which helps to make the lyrical content pass unnoticed as the song digs its way under people's skin . . . and that it did. One of the earliest pop songs to tackle the issue of land rights, which were hardly on white Australia's radar in 1982, it went to No. 2 in the charts and won best debut single at the *Countdown* Music Awards.

As to be expected, once the message of the song became clear not everyone was on board. Howard remembered a taxi driver in Alice Springs saying how much he hated 'Solid Rock' and hoped he never ran into the songwriter again. According to Howard, even some First Nations people had misgivings about the song: 'Archie Roach told a beautiful story about the first time he saw Goanna on *Countdown* performing the song,' Howard told the ABC, 'and all these fellas from the Charcoal Lane days [the name of a street in Fitzroy that became a community hub for indigenous people in the 1980s] going "What would these whitefellas know about anything?" An

old fella said to them: "Hang on, when was the last time you had a whitefella sticking up for us blackfellas?" and Archie says "We couldn't think of one."'

Howard was inspired to write 'Solid Rock' after he'd gone to a doctor feeling severely debilitated from touring and looking after his young family. The doc's prescription was to take a break, so Howard travelled to Adelaide, boarded the Ghan and headed for Uluru. 'I was camping there and it was a very powerful experience,' he said. 'I went to a corroboree and I was deeply moved – it was amazing to be in that landscape. Then I went back to Alice Springs and saw the carnage of colonisation: the grog, the violence and the dispossession. I'd started writing "Solid Rock" at Uluru but it became a very different song in Alice Springs.'

Given the band never thought there'd be much interest in the song in Australia, it came as a surprise that 'Solid Rock' made the American *Billboard* charts, peaking at No. 61. This was no mean feat for a band that hadn't set foot in the country, though the US label wanted them to fix that quick smart. However, the band said 'No.' 'Maybe it's a great opportunity missed, but I really don't think we were ready for it at the time and I don't think we would have survived,' Howard said.

It turned out that survival was also a problem for the band in Australia. 'Solid Rock' had pegged them as a political band, though Howard felt 'a great deal of the music deals with very personal and day-to-day situations as well as those larger concerns'. The band rebelled against being put in a box, and released their second album *Oceania* in 1985. The album made it to No. 29, but Howard saw the writing on the wall and left the band later that year. 'We tried to change and stop being so commercial, but we changed too much and it failed,' Howard said. 'We put so much energy and money into the second album and it was a flop. We never recovered from that.'

168 AUSSIE ROCK ANTHEMS

CHAPTER 29

SHADDAP YOU FACE

JOE DOLCE MUSIC THEATRE

People always refer to Joe Dolce as a one-hit wonder because of this song, which went to No. 1 for eight weeks in 1980, but it's not true. In fact, he's a two-hit wonder – if such a category exists. In 1981 his single 'If You Want To Be Happy' went to No. 7, but no one ever remembers that song.

Born in Ohio in 1947, Dolce moved to Melbourne in 1978. A year later he released his first single, which wasn't 'Shaddap You Face'. He self-financed the single 'Boat People', about the plight of the Vietnamese refugees heading to Australia. Then, as now, the idea of refugees heading to our shores was a divisive issue and it was certainly a subject people didn't want to hear a song about. Dolce ended up donating most of the copies of the single to the Melbourne Vietnamese community as gifts.

In Melbourne, Dolce was playing on the cabaret circuit as the one-man show Joe Dolce Music Theatre. He began working up this song based on what his grandparents said all the time: 'What's the matter, you?' or 'Eh, shaddap.' 'The words used in the song I heard in my house every day,' Dolce said. 'It seemed natural to me to put them to music.'

Once released it turned an unknown into a star: for a while anyway. With the song going to No. 1 in eight other countries, including the UK, the money started rolling in. Dolce bought a massive TV for his house and a Mercedes to drive around town and ended up burning through the 'Shaddap You Face' money in two years. Aside from cars and TVs he overspent on recording new songs, including the 1981 album *Christmas In Australia* on which he spent $120,000, three times what most albums at the time cost to make. It climbed no higher than No. 92.

Dolce had to sell the Merc, and another car was repossessed while he was in a radio station doing an interview. Years later he could see he got swept up in his 15 minutes of fame. 'What happened with the fame thing was that I got lost trying to live up to what the market was,' he said. 'If you build up your success slowly you change your self-image along the way, but I almost felt like I'd done something I shouldn't have.'

His most famous tune never went away, though for many it was dismissed as an irritating novelty song. In the UK it was voted as the worst No. 1 in history. 'I have seen this kind of thing said about the song before,' he said. 'It just keeps people talking about it and playing it, which is just fine with me.' He does, however, bristle at the branding of it as a novelty song, and with good reason. To Anglo ears it's a song where a guy sings in a funny accent, but to Italian migrants it's a song about *them* sung by one of their own at a time they didn't see or hear themselves represented in popular media. It was the groundbreaker for the ethnic Australian humour of Wogs Out of Work and others.

Journalist Craig Mathieson noted this in 2001 when the Australasian Performing Right Association released a list of the 10 best Australian songs. 'Shaddap You Face' didn't make the list and Mathieson wondered why, noting it was much more than a novelty song. 'It summed up the change in Australia when multiculturalism displaced the derogatory label "New Australian", when colourful Immigration Minister Al Grassby regularly graced the national stage and SBS was about to take to the air. It caught a social current and gave voice to it in about three minutes.'

Dolce didn't go away after the success of 'Shaddap You Face' either: he kept performing and kept releasing new music. He's written an oratorio and poetry that has been shortlisted in several Australian poetry awards, created several stage shows and even co-wrote a song that ended up on the soundtrack of the Arnold Schwarzenegger film *The Terminator*. It's played early on when the terminator is killing off all the Sarah Connors: one of them is in her kitchen listening to Dolce's song on her headphones when Arnie shoots her.

CHAPTER 30

I STILL CALL AUSTRALIA HOME

PETER ALLEN

The thing about some of the songs that go on to become Australian anthems is that they were never hits in their time. That they've left a lasting impression decades after their release would lead you to assume otherwise, but their impact was felt in the years after their release. Peter Allen's 'I Still Call Australia Home' is a case in point. First played in Melbourne on the last night of his 1980 Australian tour, it was released as a single that year and proceeded to *not* shoot up the charts. It only reached No. 72 in Australia, though it was one of those songs that was able to ride the wave when Australia became the flavour of the month overseas.

'He wrote it when he was here in Australia,' Margaret Mitchell, curator of a Melbourne Peter Allen exhibition, told the Sound As Ever podcast. 'He'd come out in 1980 with a show called *Up In One*, which was a concert performance that he did in New York and LA and then brought to Australia. And while he was here he expressed the sentiment to the audience that "I still call Australia home."'

Apparently a Festival Records executive suggested Allen write a song with that title, so he did that during intermissions on the show. 'It was him being back home and him communicating to his people here that he was still an Australian. That he was living overseas and leading a life in New York and California but he was essentially an Australian.'

'I Still Call Australia Home' gained a new lease of life when Qantas adopted it as their theme song in 1987. The original version was sung by Allan Johnston from ad agency MoJo, who was responsible for the legendary World Series Cricket 'Come On Aussie' jingle. The airline revisited the song throughout the 1990s and 2000s, featuring a children's choir singing in front of Uluru.

That 2000 choir ad led to a marriage: Paul and Ell Van Der Toorren first met when they stood next to each other in the choir. 'We talked a little and I had a crush on Ell,' Paul said, 'but was too shy to do anything about it. We didn't realise then but we lived a couple of suburbs from each other in Melbourne.

We reconnected a few years later through a mutual friend.' Paul proposed to Ell at Uluru after Qantas helped come up with a ruse to get her there by telling her they were filming a documentary.

The song returned in 2022 after COVID-19 restrictions about air travel were relaxed, with a star-studded campaign featuring Kylie Minogue, Hugh Jackman, Adam Goodes, Ash Barty and the Bangarra Dance Theatre.

Another of Allen's iconic songs is 'Tenterfield Saddler', which tells the story of his grandfather George in the first verse, his father Richard in the second and himself in the third. It has led to the regional New South Wales town occupying a strong place in Allen's life story, despite the fact he only lived there for the first six weeks of his life. Allen grew up in Armidale, which clearly doesn't work anywhere near as well in a song as Tenterfield does. ☀

CHAPTER 31

My People

THE PRESETS

★ ★ ★ ★ ★ ★ ★ ★ ★

Setting a serious political message to a banger of a tune is one surefire way of sneaking under people's radar. They hear the groove and get attached to the song, then end up singing along without initially realising what they're singing about. Maybe the message of the lyrics sinks in and, some time later, the meaning behind those words hits them. By that time they're already attached to the song.

That's the case with The Presets's 'My People'. Julian Hamilton and Kim Moyes formed the band in 2003 and established themselves on the live scene. With the release of their 2008 album *Apocalypso* they stepped it up a gear. The album debuted at No. 1 and remained in the top 40 for more than a year. It went gold in just two weeks and ultimately reached triple platinum status.

Released several months before *Apocalypso*, 'My People' was the first single spun off from the album and it went to No. 1 on the club charts and No. 14 nationally. It's likely not too many people picked up on the lyrics, which were about asylum seekers

being locked up. 'I think it's an amazing feat for a song that's meant to be out there for you to go out and sweat to and have fun to,' Moyes said, 'to actually have some depth, to actually cause a little bit of thought and even spark up a little bit of controversy.'

Moyes admitted, though, that their record label was worried the song would be a hard sell because of the subject matter. 'I remember when we played it to our record company and they were like, "We love it but how the heck are we going to get this on the radio?"' he told *Rolling Stone*. 'There was even doubt about how much triple j would get behind it, let alone any commercial station.'

Triple j listeners certainly embraced the song. Despite it being released in December 2007, just over a month before the voting for the Hottest 100 closed, 'My People' came in at No. 18. It got some attention at the ARIA awards too, being nominated for best single and best video and winning the latter.

It's easy to understand why: the song is a banger. The thumping beat of the bass and drums hit clubgoers in the chest when the song got a spin, making it a song they'd both hear and feel. Then there's the call to 'scream if you're with me', which would have seen those in the club doing exactly that thanks to the quality of the song and perhaps some artificial euphoria created by a certain substance or two. Even if you're not at the club, the bass and drum beat make you want to turn it up and see just how much your speakers can take.

Hamilton was responsible for the lyrics. 'We felt it was important to write a song that would hopefully show our overseas fans that not all Australians necessarily shared the same views as the people running the country,' he said. 'We write songs about our disaffection for the government; songs about gay rights; songs about the media's demonisation of youth – but I don't think anyone thinks of The Presets as a protest band. We're a party band.'

CHAPTER 32

Howzat

SHERBET

When a band loses one its main songwriters things are supposed to get worse, not better. In 1976 Clive Shakespeare – who, along with keyboard player Garth Porter, had written the band's hits – left Sherbet, having had a gutful of the never-ending pressure to write new songs and of the crowds of teenaged girls who followed him everywhere. 'I couldn't even go out the front of my house because there were all these girls just hanging on the fence,' Shakespeare said. 'There was always a deadline for Garth and me – another album, another tour. When it did finally end, I was relieved more than anything because I had had enough.'

As far as the band was concerned, they didn't miss a beat. Bassist Tony Mitchell stepped into the breach to help Porter, and one of their first efforts came about while they were sitting in the music room of Porter's house in Rose Bay. Mitchell came up with a slinky bassline that, surprisingly, still hasn't been used as a sample by any Australian hip-hop or dance acts, and they built a song around it: a song inspired by manager Davies telling them they should write a song about cricket. After all, this was a band that reportedly carried a cricket kit with them on tour.

That song was, of course, 'Howzat', and it still causes Porter to cringe. 'The lyrics are appalling,' he said, 'and that was all me. I'm the guilty party. I suppose they're part of the package of the song now, but when I read them in black and white I think, "Oh, my god, a six year old could have written that."'

Porter may have hated it but Australia loved it: 'Howzat' became the band's second No. 1 single after 'Summer Love'. It hit that same spot in New Zealand, went the top 10 in the UK and South Africa and was the only Sherbet single to chart in the US, where it reached No. 61. The song created enough buzz that the band made the cover of the most definitely not music-oriented *The Bulletin*. The news magazine suggested Sherbet was at the vanguard of Australian bands set to make waves overseas, and especially in the UK.

'In recent months Australasian rock has begun to surface as a major force with the emergence of bands like AC/DC, Little River Band and Split Enz,' *The Bulletin* journalist Camilla Beach wrote. 'And spearheading this invasion is Sherbet, the first new Australian band to break into the British charts since the Bee Gees turned disaster ("New York Mining Disaster") into success nine years ago.'

This was still the era of the cultural cringe, when Australians didn't think anything they created was truly worthy until someone from overseas told them it was – hence the surprised tone that some of our bands might have some overseas success.

The standout part of 'Howzat' is the supremely funky bass line from Mitchell that kicks off the track. It's slinky, it swings, it provides the entire groove of the song and it's just begging to be sampled. The popularity of a song about cheating shouldn't be taken to mean that Australians are fond of some extracurricular hanky-panky. Given 'Howzat?' is the appeal a bowler makes to the umpire, there are probably plenty of people who figure it's a cricket song.

Ironically, the success of 'Howzat' was the beginning of a slow decline for Sherbet. The hits started to fade away as the band's teenage fans grew up and looked for something more serious and the younger siblings of those teen fans craved their own rock stars to idolise. Just a few years after 'Howzat' brought the band international attention Sherbet broke up. A reformation of sorts a year later as The Sherbs saw them opt for a new-wave sound. While the songs were some of the best Sherbet/Sherbs released there wasn't a lot of interest in them, so the band packed it in again in 1984. In later years the booming nostalgia market saw the band reform as Sherbet for a few shows. 💥

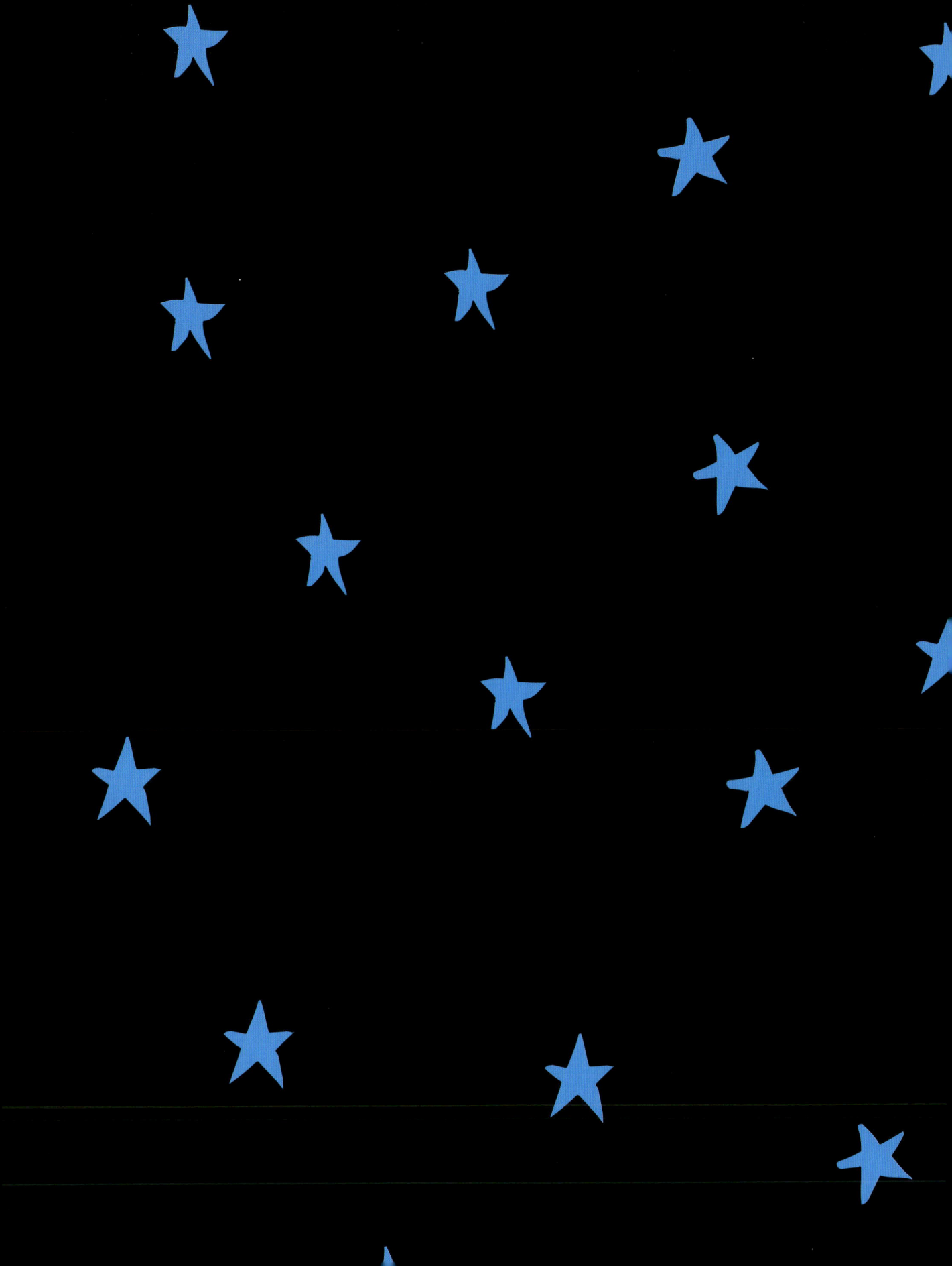

CHAPTER 33

Buy Me A Pony

SPIDERBAIT

Throughout the 1980s and early 1990s there were two distinct music worlds in Australia: one was known as mainstream and the other called 'alternative'. While alternative went on to describe a genre of music, at the time it got its name simply because those songs and bands were an alternative to what was being played on commercial radio. There were even two separate charts for the two worlds, because the idea that a band from the alternative world could cross over into the mainstream was ridiculous . . . until Nirvana came along and blew things apart. In the wake of 'Smells Like Teen Spirit', record labels saw there was money in these weird, loud alternative bands they'd ignored for so long and they waded into the world with the aim of signing up anyone they could.

One of those bands was Spiderbait, made up of friends Janet, Kram and Whit from the New South Wales Riverina town of Finley. Their full names are Janet English, Mark Maher and Damian Whitty and their

188 AUSSIE ROCK ANTHEMS

major label debut *The Unfinished Galleon Of Finley Lake*, named for an incomplete beautification project in their home town, was released in 1995 and went to No. 14, spinning off a few singles played by triple j.

Late the following year came a single from their new album *Ivy And The Big Apples*. Clocking in at 1.44 minutes, 'Buy Me A Pony' was about the thirst of the big record labels for the alternative world. 'That song was kind of like a comic-book version of how bad it can be,' songwriter Kram explained. It was released at a time when alternative music fans had had a gutful of the big guys stomping around their patch and taking away their favourite bands. 'They were really worried their music was going to be stolen from them and butchered by the commercialism of the music industry,' Kram said. 'That's one of the main reasons that song struck a chord.'

BUY ME A PONY

That it certainly did. The song took out the top spot in the triple j Hottest 100, the first time an Australian band claimed the crown. 'After three years of doing year-specific Hottest 100s we were still sitting back [in 1996] waiting for an Australian song to reach number one,' triple j music director Richard Kingsmill said, 'and we were thinking, "Oh, it's still years away for a Hottest 100 song that's Australian." But it wasn't!'

Spiderbait's win paved the way for other Australian artists to finish in top spot: The Whitlams, Powderfinger, Alex Lloyd, Jet, Bernard Fanning and Augie March are among the other local acts to reach No. 1 on the yoof radio network. Oddly enough, 'Buy Me A Pony' didn't fare that well on the charts. Its high point on the ARIA charts was No. 45, but with the increased profile that 'Buy Me A Pony' brought the band the accompanying album reached No. 3.

The band finally reached the top spot in the ARIA charts in 2004 with a cover of the song 'Black Betty'. That tune reached so many people it prompted the band to release a greatest-hits collection the following year, because a lot of the 'Black Betty' fans mistakenly figured Spiderbait was a new act that had just released its first single.

CHAPTER 34

Can't Get You Out Of My Head

KYLIE MINOGUE

Even though she didn't record this song, 'Can't Get You Out Of My Head' has become a bit of a stone in the shoe for Sophie Ellis-Bextor. There is a persistent suggestion that songwriters Cathy Dennis and Rob Davis offered this song to her and she turned it down, but Ellis-Bextor insists the first time she heard the song was on the radio. 'I'll tell you my story, but it won't make any difference to the folklore,' the singer told Double J. 'The rumour is that I was offered that song and I turned it down. But it's actually not true. But it doesn't matter. It doesn't matter that it's not true. I've always said what the truth is, but I don't think anyone cares. I promise you it will make no difference.'

Dennis and Davis were put together by Universal Publishing in 2000 to work on some songs, and the second one they wrote was 'Can't Get You Out Of My Head'. 'It was a very natural and fluid process,' Dennis said. 'The whole thing – and it does annoy me, as it will annoy others – was written in about three and a half hours.' Someone who *did* knock it

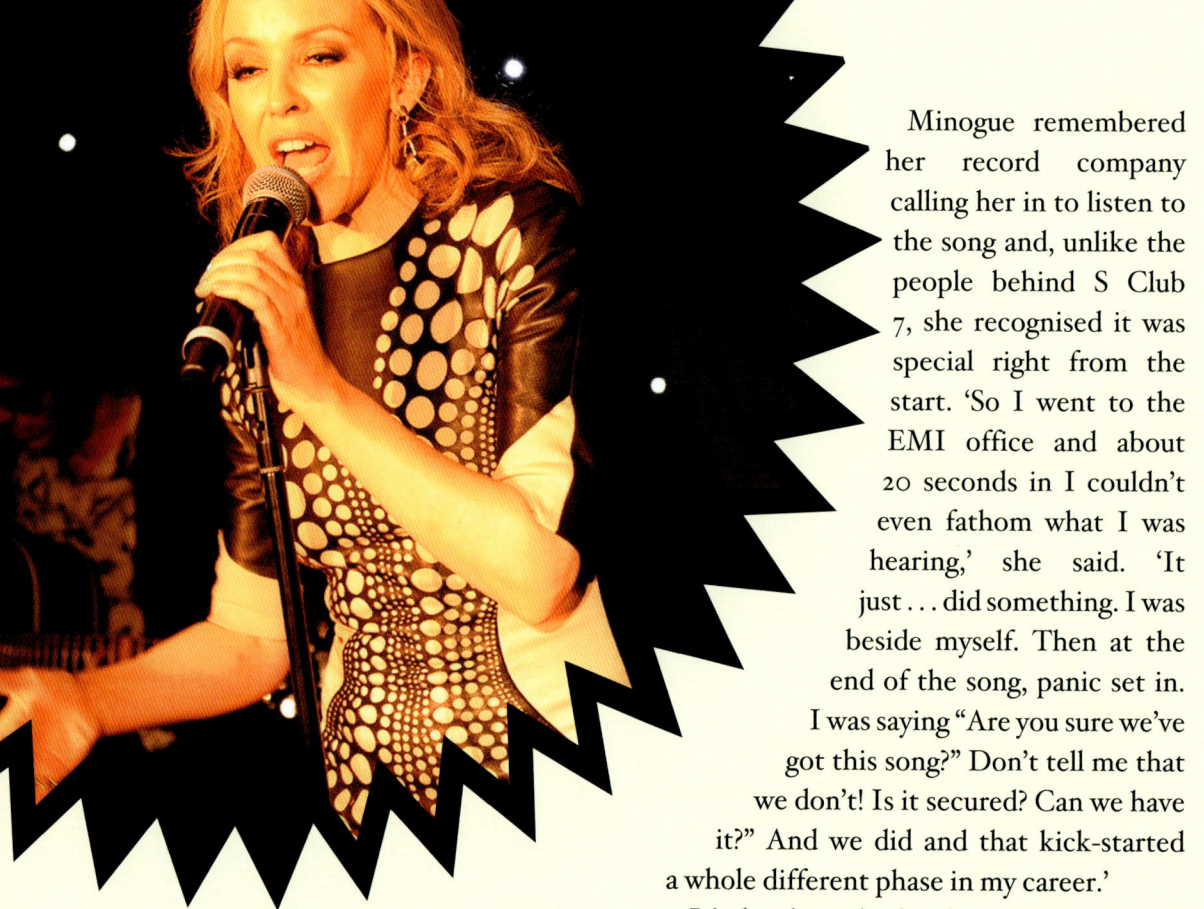

back was the managers of S Club 7, who no doubt were kicking themselves as they watched the song go to No. 1 all over Europe.

The insanely catchy song doesn't follow any of the standard rules of songwriting: there are no verses and the song is basically a chorus and a whole series of la, la, las. 'We had the "can't get you out of my head" bit,' Dennis said, 'and we had the bridge, but it needed another hook and that was the la las. We knew it didn't need another lyric, so I just went "la lala".'

Minogue remembered her record company calling her in to listen to the song and, unlike the people behind S Club 7, she recognised it was special right from the start. 'So I went to the EMI office and about 20 seconds in I couldn't even fathom what I was hearing,' she said. 'It just... did something. I was beside myself. Then at the end of the song, panic set in. I was saying "Are you sure we've got this song?" Don't tell me that we don't! Is it secured? Can we have it?" And we did and that kick-started a whole different phase in my career.'

It's hard to think of a more accurately named song than 'Can't Get You Out Of My Head' because it's what is known as earworm: a piece of music that gets stuck in your head long after it's stopped playing (though teenage boys had trouble getting the accompanying music video out their heads thanks to the very, very low-cut top Minogue wore). A look over at Spotify shows it's been played more than 379 million times, leaving 'The Locomotion' for dead at just 49 million times. Its sophisticated robo-disco sounds helped Minogue make a career change into a more 'serious' artist – that is, one the music critics liked – and may have

even opened the door for the success of the pop-electro sounds of Daft Punk.

It turned out that Minogue's radar for a hit song wasn't always perfect. Two years after 'Can't Get You Out Of My Head' Dennis wrote another song that she offered to Minogue, but the Australian singer knocked it back. Instead, Britney Spears got to record 'Toxic' and watch it reach the top of the charts all over the world. 'I wasn't at all angry when it worked out for her,' Minogue said. 'It's like the fish that got away. You just have to accept it.'

CHAPTER 35

What About ME

MOVING PICTURES

Moving Pictures frontman Alex Smith knew 'What About Me' had changed the fortunes of the band when he went out to get breakfast on the Monday morning after the song had appeared on *Countdown*. 'We were in Melbourne on tour and the next morning I wandered down Fitzroy Street to get breakfast in the usual place, and we were getting mobbed by people and it was really, really weird. It was kind of like "Hey, I was here yesterday and nobody did this."'

The band formed in 1980 and built a following on the live circuit by playing up to 12 gigs a week, this in an era when there were enough venues around to do that sort of thing. They signed a record deal and released their debut album *Days Of Innocence* in October 1981, along with the debut single 'Bustin' Loose'. For the first few months of the release the album couldn't crack the top 40, but that changed with the January 1982 release of 'What About Me'. Songwriter Garry Frost got the idea for the song when he ducked out for a sandwich on his lunch break from his day job and saw a small child waiting at the counter not being noticed by anyone.

The lyrics speak to the downtrodden and ignored, whether they be the little kid standing at the counter whom no one sees

or the female shop assistant stuck behind the counter while it seems life is passing her by without a second glance. It's not a song about greed, about wanting a handout; it's about having had enough of everyone else taking everything first. They just want a fair share, a fair go.

The band didn't quite realise what they had on their hands with this song, and it took album producer Charles Fisher's prodding to get them to record it. He'd heard Frost and Smith tinkering with the song in the studio and immediately knew it needed to go on *Days Of Innocence*, and he was right. 'What

AUSSIE ROCK ANTHEMS

About Me' sat at No. 1 for six weeks, became the second-highest–selling single of 1982 and won single of the year at the *Countdown* Music Awards. It stoked interest in the debut album, which also hit No. 1 and went platinum three times over.

The song charted in the US, the country that ultimately killed off the band. Moving Pictures scored a spot on the mega-selling *Footloose* soundtrack album, performing the song 'Never'. The band signed to Elektra subsidiary Network Records but a reshuffle at the label saw the band fall through the cracks, unloved and unpromoted, just when they were about to start a US tour opening for the likes of REO Speedwagon and Hall & Oates. Also, there was something hinky going on at Network: fellow signing Irene Cara of *Flashdance* soundtrack fame took the label to court around that time for withholding royalties, eventually winning a $1.5 million settlement.

The US experience was the beginning of the end for Moving Pictures. In 1983 they released their second album, *Matinee*, which didn't replicate the success of their debut. Three years later they called it quits, releasing the live album *The Last Picture Show*.

Their biggest hit became an Australian classic, getting a second life in 2004 when *Australian Idol* runner-up Shannon Noll released it as his first single. Like the Moving Pictures's version back in 1982, Noll went to No. 1. It was a likely catalyst for Moving Pictures to get back together a year later and play the old favourites, though the by-now British-based Smith had to figure out how to play them. 'I had to relearn the songs,' he said, admitting he didn't even have any of the band's albums at home. 'They were songs I wrote when I was 18 . . . That was a couple of lifetimes ago so it was a bit weird, but [when you relearn] the songs you start thinking, "Hey, that's not bad, we were all right."'

WHAT ABOUT ME

CHAPTER 36

SOMEBODY
That I Used To Know

GOTYE

Gotye is too polite to name her, but there is a female singer who feels rather foolish for pulling out of the recording session for 'Somebody That I Used To Know'. The song looks at the breakdown of a relationship from what initially seems like it's going to be the guy's perspective. A lot of Gotye's vocals are delivered in almost a mumble, as though we're hearing the thoughts he keeps in his head rather than saying to his ex-partner. However, more than halfway through the song the female perspective comes and we find out the guy isn't exactly blameless in the break-up, which actually adds to the sadness of the song.

That female perspective is delivered by New Zealand singer Kimbra, who was a last-minute replacement after someone else pulled out. Gotye, who his family know as Wally De Backer, had tried his girlfriend Tash Parker, but their real-life happiness meant the bitterness of the song didn't really work. 'There was a vocalist who was quite high profile in Australia who was all set to do it,' Goyte said, 'and then cancelled the night before we were going to do the vocal session. In fact, we met at a festival months later and she was just like "Maybe that was a mistake."'

The song, which appears on his 2011 *Making Mirrors* album, was a struggle to finish. Gotye said it held up the completion of the album by five months, and not just because of the change in female singer. He had also been finding the lyrics a problem: he had the two verses and a chorus but couldn't work out where to take it from there. 'For the first time I thought, "There's no interesting way to add to this guy's story,"' he said. 'It felt weak.'

That's where the idea to include the female perspective came from, which opens the song up and gives a fresh angle to the story. However, Kimbra didn't think it was going to be anywhere near as big as it

was. 'I knew it was special, but I honestly thought it was going to be, like, a track-six ballad on the record,' she told the Switched On Pop podcast. 'It's funny when record-label people tell me, "I always saw it coming. I knew it immediately when I heard the song," and I'm like, "Well, damn, you knew more than me 'cause I didn't. So maybe you guys are way smarter than me."'

No matter how smart those record-label guys think they are, it's hard to believe anyone predicted the incredible success of 'Somebody That I Used To Know'. It went to No. 1 in more than 30 countries, including the holy grail of the US *Billboard* charts, and sold more than 20 million copies. The year of its release it won five ARIA awards and was named Record of the Year at the Grammys, where it also won the Grammy for Best Pop Duo.

While Gotye made serious elephant bucks out of this record, a chunk of the songwriting royalties went to a musician who had been dead for a decade when the song was released. Gotye gave Brazilian guitarist Luiz Bonfá a co-writing credit because the distinct yet simple guitar from the song came from Bonfá's song 'Seville', which is immediately obvious the moment you listen to that song. 'That Luiz Bonfá sample directly prompted the first line of lyrics,' Gotye told *Billboard*. 'The back and forth left me thinking about these different break-ups and different relationships over the year, and the lyrics flowed from there.'

There's another sample in there from another song, but that one didn't require any songwriting credit. The xylophone riff in the song is basically the tune of the nursery rhyme 'Baa Baa Black Sheep'. It wasn't subconscious either: Gotye knew where it came from. 'I [almost] stopped myself because I thought, "Is this too cute?"' he said. 'But in the end it had a rhythm and form. Maybe the reason it cuts to the core of people is because of something in childhood. The song is very much about reflection: the whole first lyric is about thinking about old relationships and how I suppose memory can be quite unreliable.'

CHAPTER 37

PRISONER OF SOCIETY

THE LIVING END

In high school Chris Cheney and Scott Owen were, musically speaking, a bit different from their peers. It was the early 1990s, and while their classmates were listening to whatever was in the top 40 Cheney and Owen were into the niche genre of 1950s rockabilly.

In 1991 they started Runaway Boys, a cover band playing Stray Cats and Clash tunes. By 1994 the pair had started writing their own material and changed the band name to The Living End, which are the words that appear onscreen to announce the end of the 1956 film *Rock Around The Clock*. The next few years were spent building their profile through the release of several EPs and a support slot on Green Day's Australian tour, apparently scored after sending a demo and T-shirt to Green Day's guitarist Billie Joe Armstrong.

In 1997 Cheney came up with the song that changed everything for the band. 'I originally tried to write "Prisoner Of Society" like an Irish jig, tapping into Dropkick Murphys or The Pogues,' Cheney said. 'It was only later on when we started jamming that we sped it up. It's basically my take on "My Generation" or "Summertime Blues". The lyrics are "screw society, screw Mum and Dad, this is young people's music," and I wanted to put that as simply as I could.'

The song came out in September 1997 on an EP with 'Second Solution' and a cover of the *Prisoner* TV show theme 'On The Inside'. Their record label was predicting big things for the band, including a No. 1, but Cheney thought they were crazy. 'We started out playing 1950s and 1960s rockabilly covers, which was a very particular kind of crowd,' he said. 'That just wasn't the mainstream, nor will it ever be. So we never expected that we would become a mainstream kind of band.'

It turned out Cheney was wrong: 'Prisoner Of Society' went to No. 4, spent more than a year in the top 100 and came in at No. 15 in that year's triple j Hottest 100. Eventually it became the highest-selling Australian single of the 1990s. The success meant record labels were keen to sign the band, leading to the release of their debut self-titled album in October 1998. 'Prisoner of Society' was rerecorded for the album, which sparked an ongoing debate as to which version was

better: the roughness of the original with its audible count-in or the more polished label-backed version.

The song gave the band its first No. 1, hanging around in the top 50 for 63 weeks. Cheney realised things were different when he started to be recognised while walking through the local shopping centre. 'It was around that time that things started to change and it would never kinda be like it was again,' he said. 'We kinda looked up to bands that had done well and were famous. All of a sudden we became one of those bands that kids were recognising on the street, which was just very strange.'

Like many other established artists, Cheney is a bit conflicted about the band's debut album. He's proud of it on the one hand, but also hears the younger version of himself and notes what he might have done better. 'If I was to make that record now, I'd be probably ashamed of it because it has the youthful naiveté and enthusiasm that I think you can only have on a first record,' he told Double J. 'You can only get away with that kind of roughness and looseness and over-the-top energy on your first record. The energy on that record kind of overpowers the songs in a way, but that's what we were all about at that point.'

CHAPTER 38

BLACKFELLA/ WHITEFELLA

WARUMPI BAND

It was only a week after Neil Murray had moved to the Northern Territory community of Papunya, four hours out of Alice Springs, that Sammy Butcher Tjapanangka came knocking. He'd heard the whitefella had a guitar. 'I showed him the guitar,' Murray said, 'and right away I could tell he could play: there was an energy there, he was gifted.' Soon after he brought along brother Gordon on drums and Warumpi Band was born. The final piece of the puzzle was energetic frontman George Rrurrambu Burarrwanga, a fan of the likes of Chuck Berry and Elvis. 'He was the best frontman that this country has ever produced,' singer/songwriter Dan Sultan said.

The band's first single, 'Jailanguru Pakarnu (Out From Jail)' was about a man coming out of jail and trying to reconnect with family, Sammy explained. Most significantly it was sung in Luritja, making it the first rock song written in a First Nations language. The idea had come from the Alice Springs–based Central Australian Aboriginal Media Association, which suggested that writing

it in Luritja would appeal to the radio station's listeners. The band had to tread carefully when singing in Luritja to ensure they weren't giving away any tribal secrets or showing disrespect. 'In language, we have to be careful what we are saying,' Burarrwanga said, 'because me, Sammy and Gordon, we all know our own law.'

Soon enough Warumpi Band were playing in places such as Sydney and Melbourne and supporting Midnight Oil on tour. In 1985 they released their debut album *Big Name, No Blankets*. The title came from a discussion after the band had appeared on *Countdown*. 'We were playing in Halls Creek the evening that it ran, so all the mob saw it and saw us on the TV that night and thought, "Gee, you must be rich, you blokes,"' Murray told *Deadly Vibe* magazine. 'And our lead singer said, "No, we only got big name, no blankets." So that's where it comes from.'

The second single from that album was 'Blackfella/Whitefella', a song Murray said had its origins in Warumpi Band's early days. He was in the minority as a whitefella in a blackfella community but was having fun playing footy and music. 'So with that and the truth of the experiences I was having in Papunya the song just came to me,' he said. 'It was like a simple but powerful message. I still wasn't sure though, so I showed it to Sammy Butcher. He said we should do it. "We're all living together now, black and white, we gotta get along." Before we recorded it our lead singer, George, suggested we include "yellafella" as well, which we did, which was right because the song went further than just blackfellas and whitefellas.'

'Blackfella/Whitefella' was never a hit even though it appeared on the 12-inch version of Midnight Oil's 'The Dead Heart', but it did develop a cultural resonance as one of the earliest songs promoting reconciliation between white and black. As well, it ensured Warumpi Band were remembered decades after they broke up. 'The band is more well known now than we ever were when we were up and running around,' Murray said in 2021. 'Over 100,000 people stream Warumpi Band every month on Spotify: we're known all over the world now, really. But that wasn't to be. You only get a small window of opportunity.' 💥

AUSSIE ROCK ANTHEMS

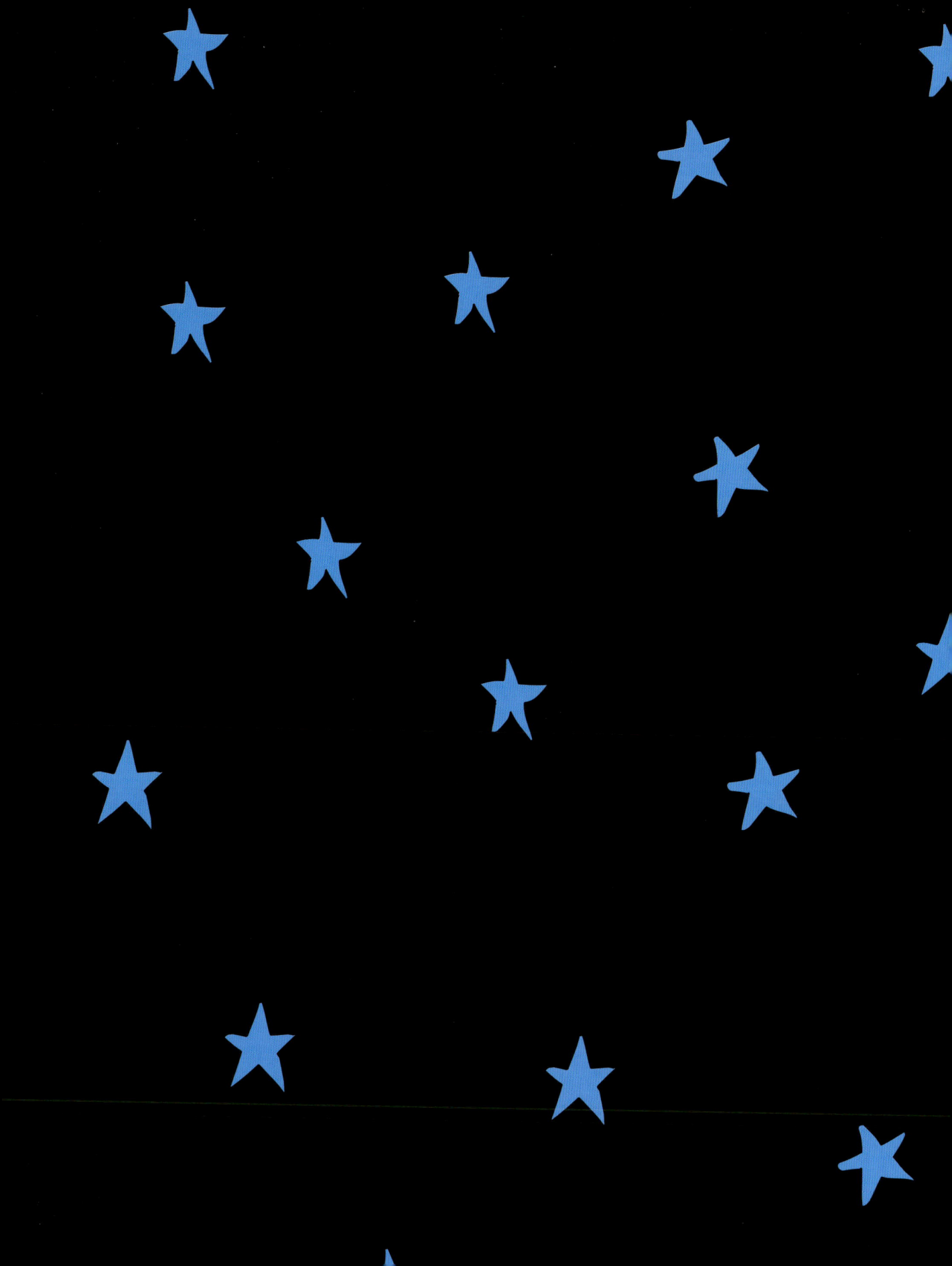

Chapter 39: Don't Change — INXS

When women are getting their hair done at a beauty salon in Elvina Avenue at Avalon it's unlikely they realise the significant piece of Australian musical history that happened right where they are sitting. In the late 1970s, mates Tim Farriss and Kirk Pengilly rented that space for their band Guinness and turned it into a recording studio. Some months later the pair invited members of another band to meet there for a jam, and in the end the band was made up of Andrew, Tim and Jon Farriss, Garry Gary Beers, Kirk Pengilly and a chap by the name of Michael Hutchence. In what is now that beauty salon was the first time the six members of INXS ever played together, and the song they recorded was a cover of 'I Shot The Sheriff'.

Initially gigging under the name The Farriss Brothers, they made the bold move of following drummer Jon from Sydney back to Western Australia; he was still in high school and had to follow his parents when they moved west. They spent eight months playing pubs and mining towns, sending Jon back to school on just a few hours' sleep. With his grades obviously slipping, he chose to drop out before he failed and the band packed up and headed back to Sydney – just in time to ride the wave of the Oz pub rock era of the 1980s.

After some time in Sydney they changed their name to INXS – their then manager was inspired by an IXL jam jar – and they released two albums on which they developed their groove-tinged sound, which was a step away from the Oz rock so prevalent in that era. The third album, *Shabooh Shoobah*, was released in 1982 and produced by Mark Opitz, who was swayed

after hearing the band play 'Don't Change' in a Wollongong leagues club. That third album was the release that really set things up for the band, with iconic singles 'Don't Change' and 'The One Thing' coming out of the album.

The album charted in the US, reaching No. 46 on the *Billboard* charts, which was the result of heavy touring in the United States as well as the introduction of *MTV*. The music video channel was hungry for content, and that opened the door for English acts and the odd Australian band because those countries were already making videos. Of course, it didn't hurt that INXS had an eye-catching frontman.

'Don't Change', the last song on the album, became the last song they played at almost every gig thereafter, aside from any encores. Oddly, they didn't play it at all at their biggest-ever gig: 1991's Wembley Stadium show in front of 74,000 fans, which was recorded for a live album. 'I don't know why we didn't play it that night,' Tim Farriss said. 'There was a very good reason; I just can't remember what it was. We often laughed about the fact that we religiously played it, last song every night, except that one night. We were like, "What the hell were we thinking?"'

'Don't Change' has been quite a popular song for other artists to cover. In 2003 Grinspoon recorded a cover on their *Panic Attack* EP, and the American hardcore/emo band AFI included a sombre, moody version as the B-side of their 'Miss Murder' single for the Australian market. The Goo Goo Dolls put a live version on their 2021 *Rarities* album.

One of the more ear-catching versions came from Bruce Springsteen during his 2014 Australian tour. With Eddie Vedder on guest vocals he had been paying tribute to Australian artists, including The Easybeats's 'Friday On My Mind' and AC/DC's 'Highway To Hell'. In Sydney he pulled out a striking

DON'T CHANGE 215

cover of 'Don't Change' with his own guitar and a horn section replacing Andrew Farriss's synth lines. Springsteen's vocals are aggressive and passionate while Hutchence's original performance was laid back, but it's still a spine-tingling cover version.

Let's be honest: the ongoing appeal of the song isn't because of the lyrics. 'I'm standing here on the ground/The sky above won't fall down': huh? When you read the lyrics it's as though someone asked ChatGPT to write a pop song. Largely speaking, the lyrics don't matter – except for one bit, which we'll get to in a minute – and it's all about the intensely catchy music. It starts out with a moody keyboard intro before the whole band launches into the song, driven by a strong guitar riff that's repeated throughout. Also, there's the harmony from Kirk Pengilly at the end, where he drags out the title of the song and turns the phrase 'Don't change' from a request into more of a hopeful plea.

This brings us to the important part of the lyric: the chorus. It sends the message that there's nothing wrong with you, nothing you need to fix, that you don't need to improve on anything to please someone else or even yourself. It's an uplifting, empowering message that you're just fine as you are: a message people still need to hear today.

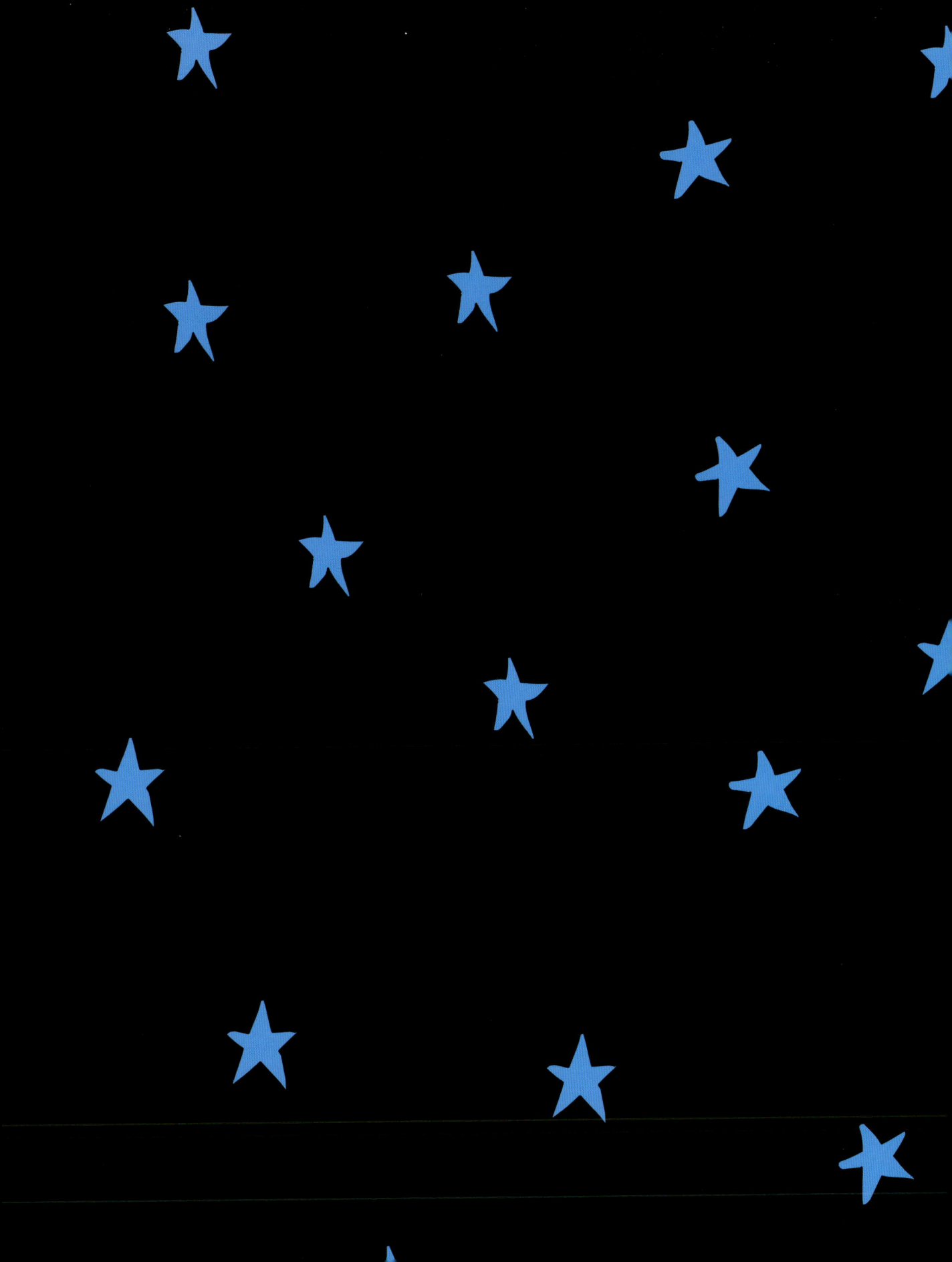

CHAPTER 40

BOYS Light Up

AUSTRALIAN CRAWL

✯ ✯ ✯ ✯ ✯ ✯ ✯ ✯ ✯

Let's clear up something right at the start: this song is not about smoking dope. Granted, it's an easy mistake to make because the title does allude to the boys smoking something and it's a rock band singing the song, and what are rock bands known to smoke from time to time? Dope. However, what James Reyne, who wrote the song, is singing about in that odd cadence of his are ciggies. It's a reference to his time in high school when he and classmates were made to do dancing classes with their sister school, and they hated it.

'We'd sit in the paddock outside school and smoke cigarettes before going in, 'cause we were so tough, and we'd smell of smoke,' Reyne said. 'So everyone thought, "Wow, they smoke." We used to make a joke before we walked in: "The boys light up. Off we go." It's just stupid. Childish.'

It's not just about smoking cancer sticks – oh, no, there's a lot more going on in 'Boys Light Up'. It's also a song about blowjobs . . . well, at least the second verse is. That's the meaning of the word

'hummers' that the unnamed woman is giving, causing all the MPs to rave. From there you might be able to guess what Reyne means by the reference to 'skin lotion'.

The song got banned by *Countdown*, which was a godsend because then everyone wanted to hear it, but the blowjobs weren't the reason for the ban. Reyne thought maybe *Countdown* felt the mother's little helper that was hidden in the drawer was a vibrator; the references to oral sex were totally missed. 'I thought the filthy bit was about the hummer and the skin lotion, and I don't even know if people know what the hell I'm talking about, if they actually realise.'

More broadly, the song satirises the middle-class world Reyne grew up in at the coastal Victorian suburb of Mount Eliza. 'I remember lots of friends of mine, their parents would have sort of cocktail parties that would get maybe a little out of hand,' Reyne said, 'and you'd hear these stories about things that went on and maybe one of your teachers from school was at the party and ended up *maybe* down the garden with someone else's wife. You know, it was all that sort of stuff. It was that kind of place.'

It's impossible to miss the name of the song, as it's repeated no fewer than an astonishing 43 times (yes, I counted them). That opens up the way for the crowd to sing along, fuelled by more than a few drinks by the time the song makes an appearance in the set. It also speaks to a certain male bonding, a certain coolness teenage boys or those in their early 20s feel when they spark up a durry. For many it may have escaped their attention that the song is about sex and blowjobs, though if they picked up on that it would have only made them like the song

even more. Musically, there's a slow groove to the song and a reggae-flecked riff that runs all the way through it.

The band's debut album of the same name was released in 1980 and quickly established Australian Crawl. It featured two co-writes from Federal Arbitration Commission justice James Robinson, the father of rhythm guitarist Brad. It raced to No. 4 on the charts and spawned four hit singles.

Their next two albums went to No. 1, which was the same place their big hit 'Reckless' landed in 1983. Things went downhill for the band from that year: drummer Bill McDonough left, then his brother and guitarist Guy died a year later and bassist Paul Williams left in 1985. That same year they released the studio album *Between A Rock And A Hard Place* but it didn't attract anywhere near the attention of their earlier recordings, so the few remaining members of the band decided enough was enough and called it a day – though not before they had to go out on one last tour to repay their debts. Australian Crawl's last release, *The Final Wave*, was a live album recorded on that tour, their second after 1983's *Phalanx*.

BOYS LIGHT UP

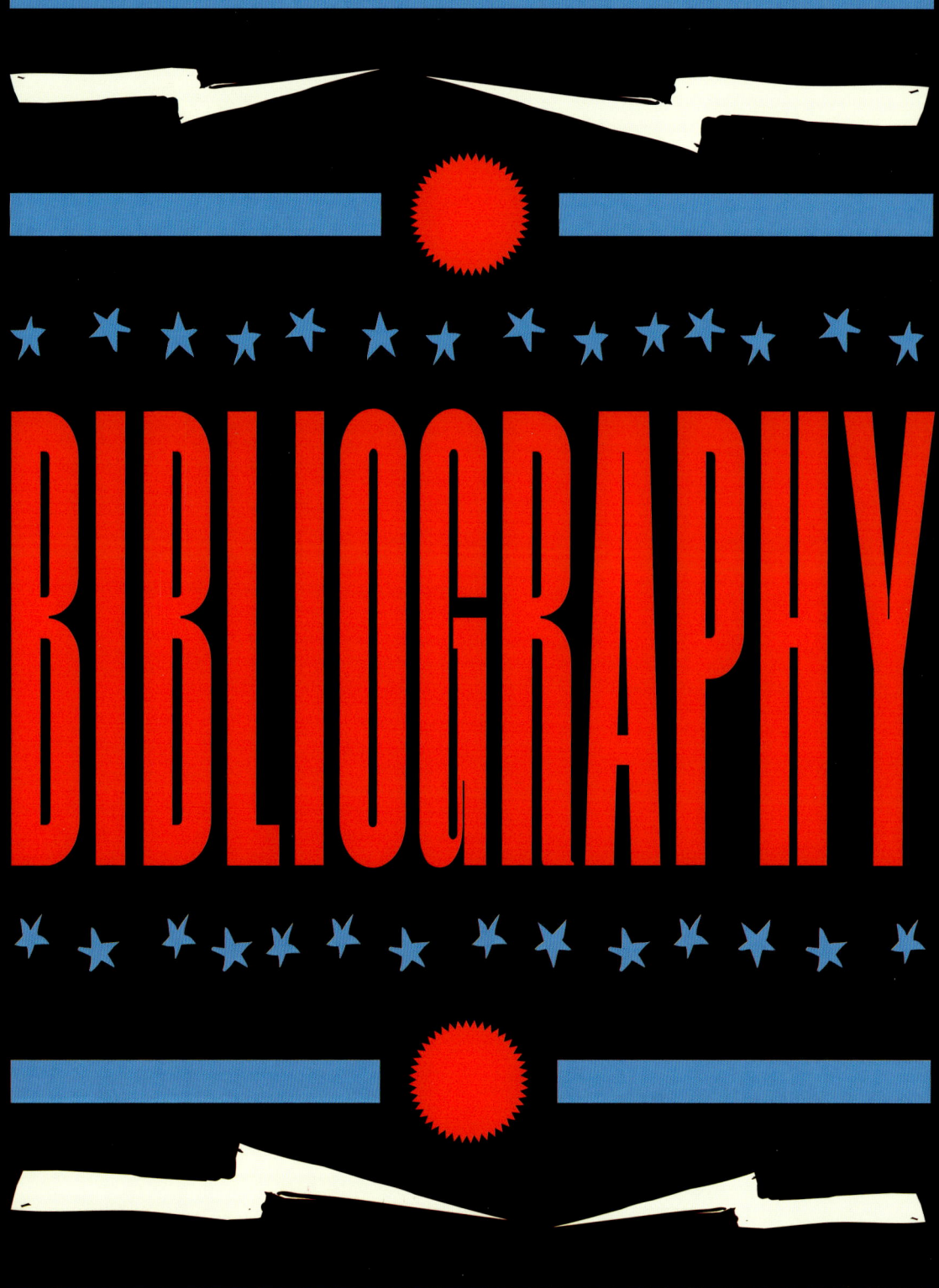

BOOKS

Amphlett, Chrissie and Larry Writer, *Pleasure and Pain: My life*, Hachette, 2009

Apter, Jeff, *Bad Boy Boogie: The true story of AC/DC legend Bon Scott*, Allen & Unwin, 2021

Apter, Jeff, *Friday on My Mind: The life of George Young*, Allen & Unwin, 2020

Apter, Jeff, *Playing to Win: The definitive biography of John Farnham*, Nero, 2016

Apter, Jeff, *The Book of Daniel: From Silverchair to dreams*, Allen & Unwin, 2018

Apter, Jeff, *Together Alone: The story of the Finn brothers*, William Heinemann, 2010

Apter, Jeff, *Up from Down Under: How Australian music changed the world*, Five Mile Press, 2013

Barnes, Jimmy, *Killing Time*, HarperCollins, 2020

Barnes, Jimmy, *Working Class Man*, HarperCollins, 2017

Bourke, Chris, *Crowded House: Something so strong*, Pan Macmillan, 1997

Bozza, Anthony, *INXS: Story to story*, Bantam Press, 2005

Bradshaw, John and Anne Souter, *Doc: The life and times of Aussie rock legend Doc Neeson*, Allen & Unwin, 2021

Cheal, David and Jan Dalley, Jan (eds), *The Life of a Song: The stories behind 100 of the world's best-loved songs*, Brewer's, 2022

Conomy, Trevor, *Down Under: The tune, the times, the tragedy*, Affirm Press, 2015

Coupe, Stuart, *Gudinski: The godfather of Australian rock'n'roll*, Hachette, 2015

Coupe, Stuart, *Paul Kelly: The man, the music and the life in between*, Hachette, 2020

Coupe, Stuart, *Roadies: The secret history of Australian rock'n'roll*, Hachette, 2018

Creswell, Toby, *Jimmy Barnes: Too much ain't enough*, Random House, 1993

Creswell, Toby, *Shine Like it Does: The life of Michael Hutchence*, Echo, 2017

Dodson, Craig, *Beds are Burning – Midnight Oil: The journey*, Penguin, 2004

Engleheart, Murray, *Blood, Sweat & Beers: Oz rock from the Aztecs to Rose Tattoo*, HarperCollins, 2010

Engleheart, Murray and Arnaud Durieux, *AC/DC – Maximum Rock & Roll: The ultimate story of the world's greatest rock and roll band*, HarperCollins, 2015

Evans, Mark, *Dirty Deeds: My life inside and outside AC/DC*, Allen & Unwin, 2012

Fink, Jesse, *The Youngs: The brothers who built AC/DC*, Ebury Press, 2013

Garrick, Matt, *Writing in the Sand: The epic story of legendary band Yothu Yindi and how their song 'Treaty' gave voice to a movement*, ABC Books, 2021

Gazzo, Jane, *John Farnham: The untold story*, Ebury Press, 2015

Gazzo, Jane and Andrew P. Street, *Sound as Ever: A celebration of the greatest decade in Australian music 1990–1999*, Melbourne Books, 2022

Horne, Craig, *Roots: How Melbourne became the live music capital of the world*, Melbourne Books, 2019

Howard, Jack, *Small Moments of Glory: A musical memoir*, Brolga Publishing, 2020

Hutchence, Tina with Jen Jewel Brown, *Michael: My brother, lost boy of INXS*, Allen & Unwin, 2018

Jenkins, Jeff, *Molly Meldrum Presents 50 Years of Rock in Australia*, Wilkinson Publishing, 2007

Kelly, Paul, *How to Make Gravy*, Penguin, 2018

Kruger, Debbie, *Songwriters Speak: Conversations about creating music*, Limelight Press, 2005

Lawrence, Michael, *Cold Chisel: Wild colonial boys*, Melbourne Books, 2017

Lawrence, Michael, *Midnight Oil: The power and the passion*, Melbourne Books, 2016

Leser, David (ed.), *Paul Kelly: The essays*, Shark Island Books, 2013

McMillan, Andrew, *Strict Rules: The iconic story of the tour that shaped Midnight Oil*, Hachette, 2017

Mathieson, Craig, *Hi Fi Days: The future of Australian rock*, Allen & Unwin, 1996

Meldrum, Molly, *The Never, Um, Ever Ending Story: and everything in between*, Allen & Unwin, 2014

Nichols, David, *Dig: Australian rock and pop music, 1960–85*, Verse Chorus Press, 2017

O'Donnell, John, Toby Creswell and Craig Mathieson, *The 100 Best Australian Albums*, Hardie Grant, 2010

Roach, Archie, *Tell Me Why: The story of my life and my music*, Simon & Schuster, 2019

Roach, Archie, *You Have the Power*, Angus & Robertson, 1994

Rogers, Tim, *Detours*, Fourth Estate, 2017

Rosen, Jody, *White Christmas: The story of an American song*, Scribner, 2003

Seymour, Mark, *Thirteen Tonne Theory: Life inside Hunters & Collectors*, Viking, 2008

Strevens, Steve, *The Jungle Dark*, Pan Macmillan, 2013

Thomas, Mick, *These are the Days: Stories and songs*, Melbourne Books, 2017

Walker, Clinton, *Buried Country: The story of Aboriginal country music*, Verse Chorus Press, 2014

Walker, Clinton, *Stranded: Australian independent music 1976–1992*, Visible Spectrum, 2021

Walker, Don, *Shots*, Black Inc., 2010

Walker, Don, *Songs*, Black Inc., 2019

Wallace, Luke and Jeff Jenkins, *Sophistopunk: The story of Mark Opitz and Oz rock*, Ebury Press, 2012

Wellington, Tony, *Freak Out: How a musical revolution rocked the world in the sixties*, Monash University Publishing, 2021

Wheatley, Glenn, *Paper Paradise: Confessions of a rock 'n' roll survivor*, Wilkinson Publishing, 2022

Yates, Bob, Rick Brewster and John Brewster, *The Angels*, Penguin, 2017

WEBSITES

abc.net.au

abc.net.au/doublej

abc.net.au/triplej

songfacts.com

NEWSPAPERS AND MAGAZINES

Adelaide Advertiser

Deadly Vibe

Geelong Advertiser

Herald Sun

Illawarra Mercury

mX

Newcastle Herald

NME

NT News

Rolling Stone

Sunday Age

Sunday Mail

The Age

The Australian

The Courier-Mail

The Sun-Herald

The Sydney Morning Herald

The Telegraph

Glen Humphries is a journalist with the *Illawarra Mercury*, spending a chunk of his time as the paper's music writer. He has also written several music books, including *Lull City*, a history of the Wollongong music scene, *Sounds Like An Ending* about Midnight Oils's *10, 9, 8, 7, 6, 5, 4, 3, 2, 1* and *Red Sails in the Sunset* albums, and one about Queen's concert at Live Aid.

He is the author of several other books published by Gelding Street Press. *Biff* and *Jack Gibson's Fur Coat* cover lesser-known stories from rugby league, while *Sticky Wickets* focuses on the summer sport of cricket.

Glen lives in Wollongong, where he tries to keep up to date with current music, although he can't help but find himself drifting back to the tunes he grew up with – some of which appear in this book. But not 'Eagle Rock': he can't stand that song.

Also, as can be seen in the pic below onstage with David Challenger and the Insiders (that's him second from the left), he goes all right on the tambourine.

The Slab: 24 stories of beer in Australia

James Squire: The biography

The Six-Pack: Stories from the world of beer

Friday Night at the Oxford

Beer is Fun

Sounds Like an Ending: Midnight Oil, 10, 9, 8, 7, 6, 5, 4, 3, 2, 1 and Red Sails in the Sunset

Night Terrors: The true story of the Kingsgrove Slasher

Healer: The rise, fall and return of Tumbleweed

Alright! Queen at Live Aid

Biff: Rugby league's infamous fights

Lull City: The Wollongong music scene 1955–2020

Little Darling: Daryl Braithwaite and The Horses

Jack Gibson's Fur Coat: Rugby league oddities and artefacts

Sticky Wickets: Australian cricket's controversies and curiosities